ENGLISH COMMUNICATION

COMMUNICATION

Q: SKILLS FOR SUCCESS

9

Susan Earle-Carlin

Series Consultants:
Marguerite Ann Snow
Lawrence J. Zwier

Vocabulary Consultant:
Cheryl Boyd Zimmerman

OXFORD
UNIVERSITY PRESS

ACKNOWLEDGEMENTS

Author

Susan Earle-Carlin earned a Ph.D. in Reading, Language, and Cognition from Hofstra University. She has taught at SUNY Old Westbury and Rutgers University and now teaches in the Program in Academic English/ESL at the University of California, Irvine. Her interests include addressing the needs of generation 1.5 students at the university and improving the communication skills of international teaching assistants. *Q* is her third ESL textbook.

Series Consultants

Marguerite Ann Snow holds a Ph.D. in Applied Linguistics from UCLA. She is a Professor in the Charter College of Education at California State University, Los Angeles where she teaches in the TESOL M.A. program. She has published in *TESOL Quarterly*, *Applied Linguistics*, and *The Modern Language Journal*. She has been a Fulbright scholar in Hong Kong and Cyprus. In 2006, she received the President's Distinguished Professor award at Cal State LA. In addition to working closely with ESL and mainstream public school teachers in the U.S., she has trained EFL teachers in Algeria, Argentina, Brazil, Egypt, Japan, Morocco, Pakistan, Spain, and Turkey. Her main interests are integrated content and language instruction, English for Academic Purposes, and standards for English teaching and learning.

Lawrence J. Zwier holds an M.A. in TESL from the University of Minnesota. He is currently the Associate Director for Curriculum Development at the English Language Center at Michigan State University in East Lansing. He has taught ESL/EFL in the U.S., Saudi Arabia, Malaysia, Japan, and Singapore. He is a frequent TESOL conference presenter and has published many ESL/EFL books in the areas of test-preparation, vocabulary, and reading, including *Inside Reading 2* for Oxford University Press.

Vocabulary Consultant

Cheryl Boyd Zimmerman is Associate Professor of TESOL at California State University, Fullerton. She specializes in second language vocabulary acquisition, an area in which she is widely published. She teaches graduate courses on second language acquisition, culture, vocabulary, and the fundamentals of TESOL and is a frequent invited speaker on topics related to vocabulary teaching and learning. She is the author of *Word Knowledge: A Vocabulary Teacher's Handbook* and Series Director of *Inside Reading*, both published by Oxford University Press.

WELCOME!

At ILSC Education Group, we take pride in delivering quality educational programs, using a dynamic approach that responds to your interests, as well as new global developments in technology and thinking. In all of our courses, we encourage you to be active participants. We teach fundamental skills in a way that engages you to learn and that inspires creativity and confidence. For more than 20 years, we have been developing and refining our teaching methods, and they have proven successful with thousands of students from all over the world.

Our goal at ILSC is to prepare you for wherever you want to go in the world by helping you achieve internationally relevant career and language skills. You'll be inspired to make learning a lifelong pursuit.

On behalf of our staff and teachers, we welcome you to ILSC. You are about to begin an exciting adventure in learning!

ILSC Global Directors and
Academic Team

SCOPE AND SEQUENCE | English Communication 9

UNIT	LISTENING	SPEAKING	VOCABULARY
1 Work and Fun **Q Where can work, education, and fun overlap?** **LISTENING 1: Voluntourism** An Online Interview (Travel and Tourism) **LISTENING 2: Science Fairs and Nature Reserves** Academic Reports (Environmental Science)	• Listen for examples • Relate examples to main ideas • Formulate pre-listening questions about a topic • Predict content • Listen for main ideas • Listen for details	• Discuss preferences and alternatives • Use intonation to express choices and alternatives • Plan a persuasive presentation • Convince listeners to opt for one choice among many • Take notes to prepare for a presentation or group discussion	• Compound words • Assess your prior knowledge of vocabulary
2 New Media **Q How do people get the news today?** **LISTENING 1: Citizen Journalism** An Online Interview (Journalism) **LISTENING 2: Pod-Ready: Podcasting for the Developing World** A Podcast (Cultural Anthropology)	• Listen for the relationships between main ideas and details • Listen for specific vowel sounds • Predict content • Listen for main ideas • Listen for details	• Use note cards • Converse about advantages and disadvantages • Convey numerical information • Conduct a survey • Take notes to prepare for a presentation or group discussion	• Using the dictionary • Assess your prior knowledge of vocabulary
3 Language **Q How does language affect who we are?** **LISTENING 1: My Stroke of Insight: A Brain Scientist's Personal Journey** A Radio Interview (Neuroscience) **LISTENING 2: The Story of My Life** An Autobiography (Cognitive Science)	• Understand inferences • Listen for events in a chronology • Predict content • Listen for main ideas • Listen for details	• Use figurative language • Practice using word stress to emphasize ideas • Imply ideas instead of stating them directly • Narrate a story • Take notes to prepare for a presentation or group discussion	• Negative prefixes • Assess your prior knowledge of vocabulary
4 Personal Space **Q How do you make a space your own?** **LISTENING 1: Environmental Psychology** A University Lecture (Psychology) **LISTENING 2: What Your Stuff Says About You** A Radio Interview (Social Psychology)	• Recognize organizational cues • Understand the overall structure of a passage • Predict content • Listen for main ideas • Listen for details	• Give advice • Practice conversational skills in an advice-giving situation • Take notes to prepare for a presentation or group discussion	• Words with multiple meanings • Assess your prior knowledge of vocabulary

GRAMMAR	PRONUNCIATION	CRITICAL THINKING	UNIT OUTCOME
• Comparative structures	• Intonation with choices	• Identify personal preferences • Categorize activities • Assess your prior knowledge of content • Relate personal experiences to listening topics • Integrate information from multiple sources	• Plan and present a school vacation in a way that will persuade your classmates to select it for their spring break alternative trip.
• Participial adjectives	• Vowel variation with *a* and *o*	• Identify people/items that fit a definition • Interpret survey data • Assess your prior knowledge of content • Relate personal experiences to listening topics • Integrate information from multiple sources	• Develop and administer a survey focused on media preferences, analyze the results, and report your findings.
• Passive voice	• Emphatic word stress	• Contrast good and bad aspects of a situation • Experiment with brain stimuli • Assess your prior knowledge of content • Relate personal experiences to listening topics • Integrate information from multiple sources	• Develop a narrative incorporating figurative language that chronologically details an incident of language loss or an inability to communicate.
• Conditionals	• Stress, intonation, and pauses to indicate thought groups	• Evaluate generalizations about groups of people • Draw conclusions from data • Assess your prior knowledge of content • Relate personal experiences to listening topics • Integrate information from multiple sources	• Role-play a talk show focused on identifying and solving conflicts centered on issues of personal space.

Unit QUESTION

Where can work, education, and fun overlap?

PREVIEW THE UNIT

A Discuss these questions with your classmates.

What are some of the factors that you consider when planning a vacation?

Can you describe a time when work or school was fun?

Look at the photo. Do you think the man is doing work or having fun? Why?

B Discuss the Unit Question above with your classmates.

Listen to Level 9(CM), Track 1 to hear other answers.

C Write the goals in the appropriate part of the Venn diagram. If you think a goal can suit education and work, write it in the center area where the circles overlap.

appreciate cultures	have fun	meet new people
~~discover new ideas~~	help society	pass tests
~~earn money~~	interact with others	play sports
~~get good grades~~	keep to a schedule	solve problems
get promoted	learn a language	think critically

 **Tip** **Critical Thinking**

In Activity C, you will complete a Venn diagram. **Diagramming** the relationships between ideas is one way of analyzing information.

Where Do Work and Fun Intersect?

Work   Education

earn money   get good grades

discover
new ideas

D In a group, compare your Venn diagrams. What does your diagram say about your attitudes toward education and work? Do you think work can be educational? Do you think education can be work?

LISTENING 1 | Voluntourism

VOCABULARY

Here are some words and phrases from Listening 1. Read the sentences. Then write each bold word or phrase next to the correct definition.

1. The senior citizens from Canada went on a cross-cultural **expedition** to explore Peru.

2. The group wanted to work with the **indigenous** people of Guatemala who are descendents of the Mayans.

3. The ads for cheap airfare, great weather, and quiet beaches were **enticing**.

4. This position calls for a wide **range** of work experience because it's a high-level position with a lot of responsibilities.

5. We will have to **validate** our visas before we are allowed in that country.

6. By learning more about the importance of keeping our culture, we work toward the **preservation** of our traditions.

7. Parents who want their children to be exposed to **diverse** groups travel to many different countries.

8. The **demographics** from the study show that 10 percent of the people there cannot read.

9. When I travel, I like to **immerse myself in** the new culture by eating at small restaurants and talking to the people there.

10. The **ecological** project involved planting more trees to protect the hillsides.

11. It's important to educate people about global issues. Seeing how other people live helps **raise awareness** of the need to protect other cultures.

12. The desire to learn a new language **prompted** me to go abroad to study for the first time.

a. _____ *(n.)* the act of keeping something in its original state or in good condition

b. _____ *(v.)* to state officially that something is useful and of an acceptable standard

c. _____ *(v.)* to become completely involved in (something)

d. _____ *(adj.)* very different from each other

e. _____ *(n.)* an organized journey with a particular purpose

f. _____ *(v.)* to make (somebody) decide to do (something)

g. _____ *(n.)* data relating to populations and groups of people

h. _____ *(adj.)* very attractive and interesting

i. _____ *(n.)* a variety of things or experiences of a
particular type

j. _____ *(adj.)* belonging to a particular place, rather than
coming to it from someplace else; native

k. _____ *(v.)* to increase knowledge of or interest in (something)

l. _____ *(adj.)* connected to the relation of plants and other
living creatures to each other and to their
environment

PREVIEW LISTENING 1

| Voluntourism

You are going to listen to an interview titled "Voluntourism" from
the Amateur Traveler website. Linda Stuart talks with show host
Chris Christensen about the nonprofit organization Global Citizens
Network (GCN).

If a *volunteer* is someone who does work without pay, and *tourism* is
the business of travel, what do you think *voluntourism* is? Write your
own definition.

_____

_____

LISTEN FOR MAIN IDEAS

 Level 9(CM)
Track 2

**Listen to the interview and answer the questions. Compare answers with
a partner.**

1. According to Stuart, what is the overall purpose of Global Citizens Network?

_____

_____

for Success

Remember that in abbreviations such as GCN and UN, each letter is pronounced separately, with stress on the final letter. In acronyms, letters are pronounced together as a word, such as TOEFL and UNICEF.

2. Some people might believe that volunteer vacations are just for wealthy people, young men, or bilingual people. What would Stuart say in response?

_____

_____

3. What effects do volunteer vacations have on both the travelers and the countries they visit?

_____

_____

LISTEN FOR DETAILS

Level 9(CM)
Track 3

Fill in this Web page for Global Citizens Network with the information you remember. Then listen again and complete it. Compare your answers with a partner.

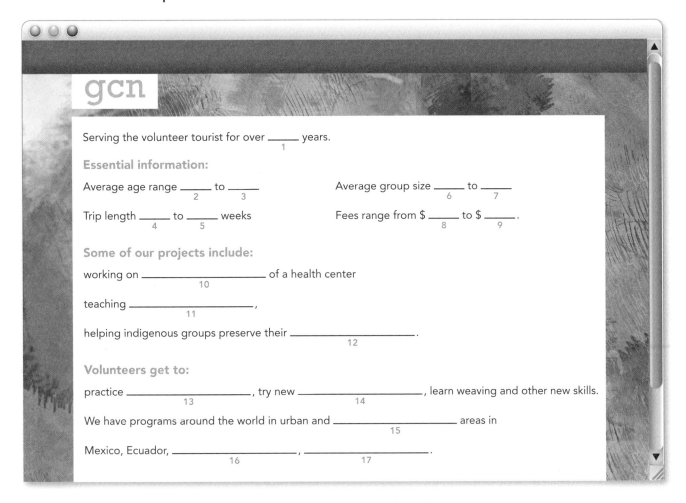

gcn

Serving the volunteer tourist for over _____ years.
                                        1

Essential information:

Average age range _____ to _____   Average group size _____ to _____
                    2   3   6   7

Trip length _____ to _____ weeks   Fees range from $ _____ to $ _____.
            4   5   8   9

Some of our projects include:

working on _____ of a health center
                  10

teaching _____,
              11

helping indigenous groups preserve their _____.
                                                12

Volunteers get to:

practice _____, try new _____, learn weaving and other new skills.
              13   14

We have programs around the world in urban and _____ areas in
                                                        15

Mexico, Ecuador, _____, _____.
                        16   17

 **WHAT DO YOU THINK?**

Discuss the questions in a group.

1. Linda Stuart says that one of the benefits of voluntourism is that it's an "eye-opening experience" and it helps people see that it's "not us versus them, but it's us all together." What does she mean by that? Do you agree?

2. In what ways has this interview been successful or unsuccessful in motivating you to take a volunteer vacation?

3. Think of a place in the world that could benefit from the contributions of volunteer tourists. What kind of work could people do there? How could it be fun?

Listening Skill	Listening for examples

In an interview, a lecture, or a report, a speaker often provides examples so the listener can understand key concepts better. Active listeners can use different strategies to notice examples.

- Listen for phrases that introduce examples: *for example, take for instance, for instance, as an example, let me give you an example, including,* and *such as.*
- Notice rising intonation that signals items in a list. A speaker who is listing examples will use rising intonation for each item in a list except for the last one. The rising intonation works like a comma to let the listener know the speaker is not finished.

 Level 9(CM)
Track 4

Listen to this example. Notice how the speaker identifies the main point and then lists examples. Pay attention to the speaker's rising intonation.

> There is a wide range of opportunities. Others include individual placement; some are in rural areas versus urban areas; others may be more of a tutoring or English teaching placements. . .

One way to take notes involving examples or other details is to write the main point on the left and examples on the right.

Main point	Examples
	individual placement
Range of volunteer opportunities	rural vs. urban
	tutoring or English teaching

A. Listen to the excerpts. Complete the chart with two examples of each main point.

Main point	Examples
1. Small-scale development projects	
2. Motivating reasons	
3. Countries GCN works in	

B. Take turns asking and answering questions with a partner about the Amateur Traveler interview.

1. What are some reasons people do voluntourism?

2. What types of people take these trips?

3. What kinds of projects do GCN volunteers work on?

4. What countries does GCN operate in?

LISTENING 2 | Science Fairs and Nature Reserves

VOCABULARY

Here are some words from Listening 2. Read the sentences. Circle the answer that best matches the meaning of each bold word.

1. The **outreach** programs bring science to rural areas so children there have equal opportunities to learn about chemistry and physics.
   a. the activity of providing a service to underprivileged people in a community
   b. designed to be not only educational but also entertaining and motivating

2. The **atmosphere** in the classroom was so energized and motivating that students didn't mind working very hard.
   a. a mood or feeling in a particular location
   b. the mixture of gases that surrounds the Earth

3. If it is a hands-on, **interactive** show, students are motivated to participate in the demonstrations.

   a. involving several performers at the same time

   b. involving both performers and audience members

4. When we visit a science **exhibit** related to elasticity, we expect to see a demonstration on how an object can stretch and bend.

   a. a written report

   b. a show or display

5. We need to choose a new **site** for that research project because the current building is too far away from our labs.

   a. a place or location

   b. a plan or idea

6. Because of the old building's historical value, the city decided to **restore** it and bring it back to life.

   a. repair; return to its original condition

   b. replace with something better

7. Schools that are famous for research such as Oxford University and the University of California **pioneer** ideas and often discover ways to cure diseases and solve problems.

   a. travel to new areas

   b. be the first to do or try something

8. The **coordinator** of the program was responsible for bringing workers together while developing that project.

   a. a person who manages

   b. a person who investigates or inspects

9. With all of the **resources** available in the library, students can find enough information for their reports.

   a. raw materials such as wood or metal

   b. things that can be used to help achieve a goal

10. The **collaboration** between environmental organizations and governments is extremely important for the success of ecological programs.

    a. the act of working together

    b. the act of working independently or separately

11. When the result of an experiment has an **impact** on science, it influences scientific ideas and may change our perspectives.

    a. a collision or accident with somebody or something

    b. a powerful effect of something on something else

12. Since we are new to the campus, we need to **familiarize** ourselves with the labs before we do any experiments.
    a. get acquainted with conditions
    b. begin a close relationship with somebody

PREVIEW LISTENING 2

The Sedgwick Reserve

Science Fairs and Nature Reserves

You are going to listen to two reports from universities, "The Cambridge Science Festival," about a science fair in England, and "The Sedgwick Reserve," about protected lands in California. They present different experiences that have been developed to engage students in science.

In your notebook, write five information questions (questions using *wh-* words) about things you would like to know about these programs.

LISTEN FOR MAIN IDEAS

Level 9(CM)
Track 6

A. Listen to the university reports. Use this T-chart and the T-chart on page 12 to take notes about the goals and outcomes of each science event as you listen.

Science Festival

Goals	Outcomes

a science fair

Sedgwick Reserve

Goals	Outcomes

B. Use your notes from the T-charts in Activity A to answer these questions.

1. The science festival at Cambridge and the nature programs at the Sedgwick Reserve have two specific goals for students beyond just making science fun. What are they?

   _____

   _____

2. What are three or four of the ways mentioned by the speakers that help their programs accomplish these goals?

   _____

   _____

   _____

3. What does *public outreach* mean, and why is it important to these universities?

   _____

   _____

LISTEN FOR DETAILS

Place these details about the science programs in the correct circles in the Venn diagram. (You can use the letters to save space.) If a detail describes both programs, write it in the overlapping area. Then listen again and correct any information.

a. botany and biology
b. in school buildings
c. students from all grades
d. geology and engineering
e. inspires interest in science
f. interactive activities
g. open to the public
h. week-long event
i. over 45,000 visitors
j. praised by teachers
k. year-long experience

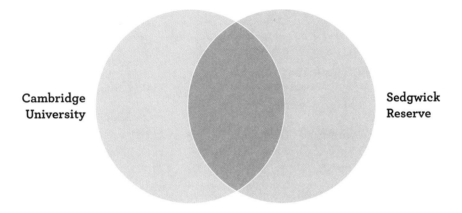

Cambridge University   Sedgwick Reserve

 WHAT DO YOU THINK?

A. Discuss the questions in a group.

1. Which of the two science programs would you most enjoy participating in? Why?

2. What should teachers be more concerned about: whether students are interested and excited about what they need to learn or whether they are learning as much information as possible about the subject?

B. Think about both Listening 1 and Listening 2 as you discuss the question.

How might going abroad to study or testing video games for a software company be considered areas where work, education, and fun overlap? Can you think of other examples?

Compounds are made up of two or more words, usually a combination of nouns, adjectives, and verbs. The most common compounds are nouns (*nature reserve*), but there are also compound adjectives (*short-term*) and verbs (*underline*).

Over time, compounds tend to become written as single words (*classroom*). Sometimes the words are hyphenated (*short-term*), and sometimes the words remain separate (*high school*) although they are considered one-word units.

Compound words are listed as separate entries in the dictionary. Since there are no strict rules for how compounds are written, it is important to check a dictionary to see if a compound is written as one word, as two words, or with a hyphen.

---

class·room 🔑 /'klæsrum; -rʊm/ *noun*
a room where a class of children or students is taught: *classroom activities* ◆ *the use of computers in the classroom*

ˈhigh school 🔑 *noun* [C, U]
a school for young people between the ages of 14 and 18
⊃ collocations at EDUCATION ⊃ see also JUNIOR HIGH SCHOOL, SENIOR HIGH SCHOOL

ˌshort-ˈterm *adj.* **1** [usually before noun] lasting a short time; designed only for a short period of time in the future: *a short-term loan* ◆ *to find work on a short-term contract* ◆ *short-term plans* ◆ *a short-term solution to the problem* ◆ *His **short-term memory** (= the ability to remember things that happened a short time ago) is failing.* ⊃ compare LONG-TERM **2** [only before noun] (of a place) where you only stay for a short time: *a short-term parking garage* ◆ *short-term patients* (= who only stay in a hospital for a short time)

Compounds are content words, so they are stressed in a sentence. Within the compound itself, there is usually a strong stress on the first word and a lighter stress on the second (*WOODlands, HOMEwork*). If the first word has more than one syllable, the stress is the same as it is in the word by itself (*DAta, DAtabase*).

All dictionary entries are from the *Oxford Advanced American Dictionary for learners of English* © Oxford University Press 2011.

A. Write the words in the right column on the correct lines.

1. computer _____   boomer

2. baby _____   reach

3. eye _____   cultural

4. out _____   ground

5. net _____   sight

6. grass _____   opening

7. senior _____   game

8. cross _____   lands

9. over _____   citizen

10. testing _____   working

B. Work with a partner. Take turns reading the compound words in Activity A aloud. Listen for your partner's stress on the first word. Check a dictionary to find out if the compounds are written as one word (with or without a hyphen) or two.

C. Complete these sentences with compounds from Activity A.

1. Realizing how much fun science can be is a(n)

   _____ experience for many teenagers.

2. Students walked through the _____ while they

   were at the Sedgwick Reserve.

3. GCN specializes in _____ for those who want to

   meet indigenous groups while traveling.

4. A small community is often the _____ for new

   ideas that later spread to larger cities if they are successful.

5. The _____ center on campus provides a place for

   students from diverse communities to meet.

6. An American born right after World War II, between 1946 and 1964,

   is called a(n) _____.

Grammar | Comparative structures

When discussing similarities and differences, comparative structures can be used with various word forms.

Word form	Comparison	Negative comparison	Intensified comparison	Comparison of equality
Adjective	clearer than more enticing than	less aware	much clearer than much less aware than	as enticing as
Adverb	faster than more slowly than	less slowly than	much faster than much more/less slowly than	as fast as as slowly as
Noun	more exhibits than more time than	fewer exhibits than less time than	many more/fewer exhibits than much less time than	as many exhibits as as much time as
Verb	travels more than	travels less than	travels much more/less than	travels as much as

Tip for Success

Even native speakers sometimes get confused when using pronouns with comparisons. Is it correct to say *Jane is taller than me* or *Jane is taller than I*? To find the answer, complete the sentence in your head: *Jane is taller than I am.* Therefore, the correct comparison is *Jane is taller than I.*

Remember when making comparisons that you must compare parallel elements.

✓ The trip to China had more stops than the trip to India.
   <u>noun phrase</u>   <u>noun phrase</u>

✗ The trip to China had more stops than India.
   <u>noun phrase</u>   <u>noun</u>

Repetition of elements in a comparison can be avoided in two ways:

1. Using a synonym of the element compared

   The Cambridge science demonstrations covered more fields than **the Stanford exhibits.**

2. Using pronouns (*this, that, these, those, the one, the ones, mine, yours, his, hers, ours, theirs, other,* and *others*)

   The meals we ate in Thailand were better than **those in England.**

A. Circle the correct answers to complete these comparative sentences. Avoid repetition in the comparative.

1. My father has traveled less than (I / me).

2. I don't like these travel options as much as (them / those).

3. The Cambridge program is shorter than the (Sedgwick one / Sedgwick program).

4. Jose's science project is more interactive than (Tim / Tim's).

5. The flight to Dubai was twice as long as (the flight to Frankfurt / Frankfurt).

6. Volunteer vacations usually cost less money than (regular trips / regular vacations).

7. Your method for solving that problem takes more time than (me / my way).

8. An expedition to China is more enticing than (England / a term in England).

Tip for Success

When making a comparison, make sure to stress the comparative words and phrases. *PHY-sics is MORE IN-ter-est-ing than CHEM-is-try.*

B. Work with a partner. Take turns reading the sentences below and then restating the comparison using a comparative structure from the Grammar Box.

1. The trip to Peru costs $5,000. The trip to Bolivia costs $5,000.

   A: The trip to Peru costs $5,000 and the trip to Bolivia costs $5,000.
   B: The trip to Peru costs as much as the trip to Bolivia.

2. A science fair sounds good. A nature expedition sounds exciting.

3. The bus trip is ten hours long. The train ride is five hours long.

4. The grasslands stretch for 50 miles. The woodlands cover 25 miles.

5. GCN needs 50 volunteers. Earthwatch needs 50 volunteers.

6. The wagon moves slowly, at five miles per hour. The tractor moves slowly, at ten miles per hour.

Choice Statements

When a list of choices is given in a series, rising intonation starts on the stressed syllable of each choice, pitch drops on *or*, and the sentence ends with a rise-fall intonation that signals the end of the choices. Listen to this example.

Level 9(CM)
Track 8

☐ With GCN, we can take an expedition to Mexico, Peru, or Argentina.

If the last item ends in a stressed syllable, glide up and down on that word. Listen to this example.

Level 9(CM)
Track 8

☐ They need to find out if that institute is in China or Japan.

Choice Questions

Questions that offer the listener two or more possible choices (or answers) have rising intonation starting with the stressed syllable in the first choice, a drop in pitch on *or*, and a rise and then a low fall (or a glide up and down) on the last choice. Listen to these examples.

Level 9(CM)
Track 8

Did they visit Cambodia, Vietnam, or Thailand?

Is it a science fair or a science camp?

If the choice question is an information question, the *wh-* clause ends with rise-fall intonation. The pitch rises on each choice, falls on *or*, and ends with a rise-fall or a glide-fall on the last choice. Listen to these examples.

Level 9(CM)
Track 8

What did they build in Mexico, schools or houses?

Where are the exhibits, in the school, at the beach, or in the park?

A. Work with a partner. Mark the intonation in these sentences and take turns reading them. Then listen and check your answers. Correct any sentences whose stress you didn't mark correctly.

 for Success

Remember, the answer to a choice question is not *Yes* or *No*; the answer should be one of the choices.

1. Who paid for the travel expenses, the students or the school?

2. Would you choose to initiate a new project or work on an old one?

3. I'm not sure if I prefer Cambridge, Oxford, Harvard, or Stanford.

4. Which adjective is best: *compelling*, *liberating*, or *enticing*?

5. You have your choice of staying in a tent, a home, or a hotel.

6. Can everyone go on a volunteer vacation, including children, teens, and adults?

B. Complete the questions. Give two choices for three of the questions and more than two choices for three of the questions. Then ask and answer the questions with a partner. Pay attention to your intonation patterns.

1. Where would you like to travel, _____

   _____?

2. What kind of ethnic food would you like to try, _____

   _____?

3. How long does it take to fly to Egypt, _____

   _____?

4. Which activities are both fun and educational, _____

   _____?

5. What kind of outdoor places do you like to explore, _____

   _____?

6. Who is the best coordinator for a trip to _____, _____

   _____?

Speaking Skill | Discussing preferences and alternatives

In a meeting or a planning session, discussion often involves expressing preferences and offering alternatives. Additionally, you might need to investigate people's past preferences to help make choices about future actions.

Here are some common expressions for talking about preferences and alternatives.

To talk about past preferences	To talk about current preferences
prefer + noun or noun phrase Students **preferred** the expedition to China.	*preference* + *is* + infinitive **My preference is to attend** a science fair.
choose + infinitive Students **chose to visit** indigenous people.	*would rather (not)* + verb I**'d rather do** something that helps society.
first/second choice + be My **first choice was** to visit a nature reserve.	*If it were up to me,* ... **If it were up to me,** we'd do an ecological study.
had hoped + infinitive I **had hoped to spend** the summer volunteering in Africa.	*I like ... more than ...* **I like** studying in my dorm **more than** in the lab.
	I'd like + verb **I'd like to explore** the idea of working abroad.

A. With a partner, take turns asking and answering these questions about the Listening texts. Use expressions for preferences and choices in your answers. Pay attention to your intonation in any choice questions.

1. Does Linda Stuart prefer the volunteering or the tourist side of voluntourism?

   A: *Does Linda Stuart prefer the volunteering or the tourist side of voluntourism?*
   B: *Stuart would rather be a volunteer than a tourist.*

2. Does Stuart's organization choose to take large or small groups of travelers?

3. If it were up to the speaker from Cambridge, would the science fair there have many more participants?

4. What does the professor at UC Santa Barbara hope to show the young students, especially girls?

5. Do you think the students in the Kids in Nature program would rather learn about plants in the classroom or at the nature reserve?

6. Do you think the children who go to the science fair will choose to become scientists and study at Cambridge?

7. Could you tell if the director's preference would be to have more visitors to the reserve?

B. Work in groups of three. Create a short role-play to present to the class. Student A is a travel agent. Students B and C want to take a trip. Student A asks B and C about their travel preferences—destination, length of trip, activities, etc. Use as many different structures as you can.

A: Would you prefer to take a relaxing vacation or go on a learning expedition?
B: My preference is a relaxing vacation.
C: Hmm. I'd like to explore the possibility of an expedition to Africa!

Unit Assignment | Plan and present a school trip

In this section, you will work with a group to plan a fun and meaningful vacation that you will try to convince your classmates to join. As you prepare your presentation, think about the Unit Question, "Where can work, education, and fun overlap?" and refer to the Self-Assessment checklist on page 24.

For alternative unit assignments, see the *Q: Skills for Success Teacher's Handbook*.

CONSIDER THE IDEAS

A. Read these two end-of-program evaluations from two people who went on a school trip to Baja, California, to study the marine and desert environments.

1.

The trip started out great. I really liked the scenery. Unfortunately, I hurt my back the second day when we spent the whole day setting up tents and digging trenches. I would have preferred more help from the teachers with that work. Then I got a bad sunburn from looking for research specimens in the desert all day, and that evening I got more mosquito bites than I have ever gotten in my life before. Next time, I would prefer to camp somewhere without mosquitoes.

I thought the project was interesting, certainly more interesting than regular classroom study, but we weren't able to collect as many specimens as we needed for our research, so we couldn't finish our project. That was pretty disappointing. Oh, and the food was worse than the school cafeteria's.

2.

This school trip was better than any other school trip I have ever taken. We worked hard (maybe harder than I have ever worked before!), saw some amazing sights, and learned a lot. I prefer this kind of hands-on learning to just reading textbooks. I think I learn better when I actually do something myself.

The only thing I didn't like about the trip was some of the other students. I think they just didn't want to be there. I'd rather do this kind of expedition with people who are as motivated as I am. Maybe you should charge more money for the trip, and then only people who really want to be there will come.

B. Compare the two experiences of hands-on vacations revealed here. What did the two participants like and not like?

C. Which do you think plays a bigger role in how much someone enjoys a trip such as this one: the person's attitude or what he or she actually experiences on the trip?

PREPARE AND SPEAK

A. GATHER IDEAS An organization has requested your help in planning a five-day alternative vacation for students over spring break. They want the vacation to be meaningful and educational, but also fun. The organization has received funding for a large group, so money does not have to be considered.

1. In a group, brainstorm trip ideas by asking one another questions. Find out preferences and make comparisons. Make notes of your ideas.

   Would you prefer to work on a science project or do volunteer work?
   Which type of trip do you think would be more fun?

2. Look at your list of ideas and choose one trip to present to the class.

B. ORGANIZE IDEAS Follow these steps to prepare your presentation.

1. As a group, complete the chart below with details about your trip.

Alternative Spring Break	
Plan	
Location	
Purpose of program	
Opportunities for fun, learning, work	
Benefits	
Travel details	

2. Choose one person in the group to present each different part of the trip plan. One person should add a summary comment about why the class should vote for your trip.

C. SPEAK Practice your parts of the presentation individually and then together as a group. Then present your alternative spring-break plan as a group to the class. Refer to the Self-Assessment checklist on page 24 before you begin.

D. After you listen to all of the class presentations, vote on which trip to take. You can vote for your own trip, but you don't have to. Your teacher may call on volunteers to explain why they chose the trip they did.

I thought the trip to Antarctica was more exotic than any of the others.

CHECK AND REFLECT

A. CHECK Think about the Unit Assignment as you complete the Self-Assessment checklist.

Yes	No	SELF-ASSESSMENT
☐	☐	I was able to speak fluently about the topic.
☐	☐	My group and the class understood me.
☐	☐	I used comparative structures correctly.
☐	☐	I used vocabulary from the unit to express my ideas.
☐	☐	I used correct intonation to question and list choices.
☐	☐	I discussed preferences and alternatives.

B. REFLECT Discuss these questions with a partner.

What is something new you learned in this unit?

 Look back at the Unit Question. Is your answer different now than when you started this unit? If yes, how is it different? Why?

Track Your Success

Circle the words and phrases you learned in this unit.

Nouns
atmosphere 🔑
baby boomer
collaboration
concept 🔑 AWL
coordinator AWL
database
demographics
exhibit 🔑 AWL
expedition
grasslands
high school 🔑
homework 🔑
impact 🔑 AWL
nature reserve
network 🔑 AWL

outreach
oversight
preservation
range 🔑 AWL
resource 🔑 AWL
site 🔑 AWL
testing ground
woodlands

Verbs
familiarize
pioneer
prompt 🔑
restore 🔑 AWL
underline
validate AWL

Adjectives
cross-cultural
diverse AWL
ecological
enticing
eye-opening
hands-on
indigenous
interactive AWL
short-term

Phrases
immerse oneself in
raise awareness

🔑 Oxford 3000™ words
AWL Academic Word List

Check (✓) the skills you learned. If you need more work on a skill, refer to the page(s) in parentheses.

LISTENING	○	I can listen for examples. (p. 8)
VOCABULARY	○	I can use compound words. (p. 14)
GRAMMAR	○	I can use comparative structures. (p. 16)
PRONUNCIATION	○	I can use intonation with choices. (p. 18)
SPEAKING	○	I can discuss preferences and alternatives. (p. 20)
LEARNING OUTCOME	●	I can plan and present a school vacation in a way that will persuade my classmates to select it for their spring break alternative trip.

LISTENING ●	identifying main ideas
VOCABULARY ●	using the dictionary
GRAMMAR ●	participial adjectives
PRONUNCIATION ●	vowel variation with *a* and *o*
SPEAKING ●	using note cards

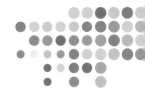

Develop and administer a survey focused on media preferences, analyze the results, and report your findings.

Q *Unit* QUESTION

How do people get the news today?

PREVIEW THE UNIT

A Discuss these questions with your classmates.

Which form of media do you turn to when you want to get the latest news? Why?

How do you judge if the information from the news is correct?

Look at the photo. What new media have appeared in the last 50 years? What changes have they caused?

B Discuss the Unit Question above with your classmates.

Listen to Level 9(CM), Track 10 to hear other answers.

C Complete the survey about news sources.

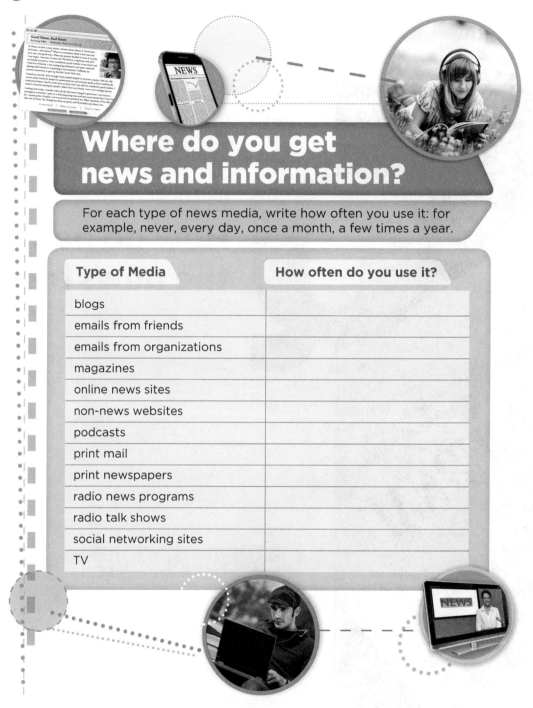

Where do you get news and information?

For each type of news media, write how often you use it: for example, never, every day, once a month, a few times a year.

Type of Media	How often do you use it?
blogs	
emails from friends	
emails from organizations	
magazines	
online news sites	
non-news websites	
podcasts	
print mail	
print newspapers	
radio news programs	
radio talk shows	
social networking sites	
TV	

D Work in groups. Share your responses to the survey. Ask and answer follow-up questions.

A: I check one blog every day. Some others I check once a week, or when they post updates.

B: Which blog do you check every day? What's it about?

LISTENING 1 | Citizen Journalism

VOCABULARY

Here are some words from Listening 1. Read each set of sentences. Then write each bold word next to the correct definition.

Tip for Success

Figuring out the part of speech (such as verb, noun, adjective, and adverb) can help you guess the meanings of unfamiliar words.

1. My parents don't like to check the news online. Their **viewpoint** is that online news is too subjective and is less reliable.

2. The **foundation** for any good news report is a strong desire to uncover and deliver the truth.

3. Ted is doing a lot of **networking** with fellow journalists because he wants to find a new job.

4. Many blogs don't seem to have a **unique** opinion about stories or events; in fact, they're sometimes copied directly from other places!

   a. _____ (n.) an underlying principle, an idea, or a fact that supports something further

   b. _____ (n.) a way of thinking about a subject; an opinion

   c. _____ (adj.) very special or unusual

   d. _____ (n.) a system of trying to meet and talk to people

5. The events were **unfolding** so quickly that the photographer was unable to capture them all on film.

6. That statement was not **accidental**. He meant to say it.

7. That reporter has a **bias** in favor of one presidential candidate, but she still writes fair and balanced reports that give equal attention to all of the candidates.

8. When reporters are held **accountable** and know there are consequences for making mistakes, they check the facts more carefully.

   e. _____ (adj.) happening by chance; not planned

   f. _____ (v.) happening at the moment; taking place

   g. _____ (adj.) responsible for decisions or actions

   h. _____ (n.) a strong feeling for or against something

9. The person who supplied the information wanted to remain **anonymous**, so we will never know who it was.

10. Don't hide the truth. Be **upfront** and explain exactly what happened.

11. My friends aren't a reliable **source** of information. They don't check facts before they repeat a rumor; they believe everything they hear!

12. My favorite **technique** for staying up to date with the news topics that I'm interested in is to subscribe to several blogs about those issues. They send updates to my email whenever there is fresh news.

i. _____ *(adj.)* with a name that is not known or made public

j. _____ *(n.)* a way of doing something, using special skills

k. _____ *(adj.)* not trying to hide what you think or do; honest

l. _____ *(n.)* a person or document that provides information

PREVIEW LISTENING 1

Citizen Journalism

You are going to listen to an interview with Robin Hamman from the website cybersoc.com. The topic is citizen journalism and the way members of the public help collect and report the news.

Check (✓) the activities you have participated in. Then listen to see if you fit Hamman's description of a citizen journalist.

☐ Written articles for a school or local newspaper

☐ Posted blog entries and responded to comments and opinions online

☐ Posted something about the news on a social networking site

☐ Uploaded photos to the Internet of people or events that seem important

☐ Posted a video to a site such as YouTube

LISTEN FOR MAIN IDEAS

Level 9(CM)
Track 11

Read the questions posed by the host of the interview. Then listen to the interview and circle the answer that best represents Hamman's response.

1. **Host:** "And I, uh, I began by asking him to define what *citizen journalism* is."
   a. Citizen journalism is news reported by someone with or without journalistic experience who is interested in the story.
   b. Citizen journalism is news reported by newspaper journalists that includes personal viewpoints and opinions of ordinary citizens.

2. **Host:** "You've been, you've been sort of involved in watching citizen media and social networking sites for a long time. How have they changed over the years?"

   a. The quality of citizen media reports has been going down steadily over the years.

   b. It is easier for people to participate in citizen media now because of easy access to technology.

3. **Host:** "Are there times where citizen journalism has really sort of taken to the forefront of, of news gathering?"

   a. The "accidental" journalist is the most common example: someone who happens to be at the scene of a news event and can report on it more quickly.

   b. Reports or news by a nonprofessional reporter can be more accurate and less biased than those by journalists.

4. **Host:** "It seems that one of the criticisms of citizen journalism is, uh, that they're not as accountable. . . . [B]logs haven't been around long enough, some of them are anonymous—how are they dealing with that concern?"

   a. This concern has caused citizen journalists to be more open and honest about who they are and what their biases are than traditional journalists.

   b. Citizen journalists who are serious about reporting the news often go on to become more educated and get journalism degrees.

5. **Host:** "What's the next step in the evolution of, of journalism and citizen journalism?"

   a. In another decade, almost all journalists will be citizen journalists.

   b. Traditional journalists will use techniques started by citizen journalists.

LISTEN FOR DETAILS

Level 9(CM)
Track 12

Listen again. Circle the word or phrase that best completes each sentence.

1. Hamman says that good journalists should check facts _____.

   a. when there is a good reason to doubt the truthfulness of something

   b. just once, but with a reliable source

   c. two or three times

2. Hamman says that some citizen journalists _____.

   a. begin by just sharing something interesting with their friends

   b. are trying to become famous through Internet exposure

   c. are motivated by money they hope to earn

3. The accidental citizen journalist who used the Internet to share information on the plane sinking into the Hudson River posted a _____.
   a. blog entry
   b. news article
   c. photograph

4. According to Hamman, when reporting the news, newspaper journalists _____.
   a. should never express their own points of view
   b. can include their own opinions and let their readers decide
   c. should cover only stories that they believe in

5. In the future, Hamman thinks we might see _____.
   a. more mainstream journalists who pick up on the techniques of citizen journalists
   b. a decline in ordinary citizen journalism as people start to lose interest in it
   c. more rules and regulations to govern the content of blogs

6. Hamman points out that journalists are using blogging, Facebook, and Twitter to reach out to _____.
   a. new audiences and advertisers
   b. new sources of information and different points of view
   c. new audiences and sources of information

Q WHAT DO YOU THINK?

Discuss the questions in a group.

1. Do you think citizen journalism could be more effective than traditional or mainstream journalism? If so, in what circumstances?

2. If fewer young people read newspapers and watch TV news these days, what can mainstream news organizations do to attract them?

3. Do you think citizen journalism would be equally popular in every country? Why or why not?

Main ideas are often stated directly. A speaker may give the main idea first and then add supporting details, or he or she might give the details first and then state the main idea. Sometimes, however, the main idea is *not* stated directly. The speaker will provide only examples, arguments, or other types of supporting information, and the listener must draw conclusions from this supporting information.

Here are some tips to help you identify main ideas when you listen to an interview, lecture, or report.

Tip for Success

A **topic** is what the speaker is talking about. The **main ideas** give a general idea of what the speaker wants to communicate to the listener. The **details** support each main idea.

- Consider the title. The title should give you the topic and often will give you an overall idea of what the interview, lecture, or report will be about. It may also give you the bias of the speaker.

☐ Blogs: A great way to share your ideas

- Listen closely to questions that a reporter or speaker asks. The questions will often lead you to the main idea of all or part of the piece.

☐ "What's the next step in the evolution of, of journalism and citizen journalism?"

- Main ideas are sometimes stated first and then followed by supporting details. They are sometimes announced by phrases such as these, but not always.

Today I'm going to talk about . . .
Let's look at three ways that . . .
A major reason for . . . is that . . .

- Main ideas can also be stated last. Summary words and phrases show that a conclusion is being drawn from supporting information.

So, that means . . .
Therefore, we can see that . . .
All of this points to . . .
These are techniques that . . .
This is the reason that . . .

A main idea statement is too broad if it is vague (unclear) or goes beyond what the speaker is trying to say. It is too narrow if it doesn't fully cover what the speaker is saying about the topic or if it sounds like a specific example.

Topic: Local News
Main Idea That Is Too Broad: TV news is not for everybody.
Main Idea That Is Too Narrow: Local reporters provide the best small-town news.
Good Main Idea: People in small towns want local news.

Tip Critical Thinking

Activities A through C ask you to **apply** the information about identifying main ideas. When you apply something, you take a concept and put it into use. In this case, you are demonstrating your understanding of the difference between main ideas and details and applying your knowledge.

A. Work with a partner. Look at these topics from Listening 1. Circle the best main idea statement for each topic and discuss why the others are too broad or too narrow.

1. The main idea of the program "Citizen Journalism" is:
   a. Citizen journalism is a new trend that allows people to share news stories.
   b. Some of the new ways people share stories are by blogging and posting messages on Facebook.
   c. It's interesting that people can write their own news stories today.

2. The main idea the speaker presents about the influence of citizen media on mainstream journalists is:
   a. Mainstream journalists should stick to what they do best.
   b. Mainstream journalists can learn new techniques and develop a more open style of reporting.
   c. Mainstream journalists might benefit from using Facebook and Twitter.

B. Work with a partner. Look at these sentences from the beginning of Listening 1. Write *M* by the main idea and *D* by the details. Then put the sentences in the order you would say them.

___ 1. But they're people who become interested in a story or an idea, and they go out and they start reporting on it and telling the world about it.

___ 2. Other times it's full of opinion and, and personal viewpoints that haven't been checked, that may or may not have any kind of foundation in truth.

___ 3. Sometimes they'll do that in the same way as, as one would hope journalists do, which is you know, gather the facts, make sure everything has been checked two or three times, and then run the story.

___ 4. Citizen media is ordinary people.

Level 9(CM)
Track 13

C. Listen to these details from Listening 1. Match the details with the main ideas they support (*a, b, c,* or *d*). Then listen again and check your answers.

1. ___   a. So, he wasn't trying to become a journalist . . .

2. ___   b. So, people are used to kind of the basic tools of home computing.

3. ____   c. So I think that's one change that we're going to see where citizen journalism and blogging is actually going to affect the, the future of journalism.

4. ____

             d. They do have a bias, they do have an opinion.

LISTENING 2 | Pod-Ready: Podcasting for the Developing World

VOCABULARY

Here are some words from Listening 2. Read the sentences. Circle the answer that best matches the meaning of each bold word.

1. New media technology is one of the key **components** of the government's plan to improve communication.
   a. mistakes
   b. parts
   c. businesses

2. The numerous **on-demand** TV and radio shows available nowadays let you watch or listen to your favorite shows whenever you want.
   a. biased
   b. popular
   c. immediate

3. Listening to the news on the radio or on a podcast is a **liberating** experience for adults who can't read.
   a. unnecessary
   b. troubling
   c. freeing

4. The podcast on food and diet was so **compelling** that soon more than 30,000 people were downloading and listening to it each day.
   a. unclear
   b. interesting
   c. common

5. In many parts of the world, radio is still a popular **medium** for getting news and information to people.
   a. a way to communicate
   b. an audio program
   c. a small machine

6. There was a **finite** amount of money, and when it was gone, the project had to be canceled.
   a. limited
   b. sufficient
   c. necessary

7. The plan to provide computers and Internet access to the rural town was not **feasible** due to limits on electricity.
   a. interesting
   b. well-known
   c. possible to do

8. Planning the two-day trip to the small village in Zimbabwe, Africa, required solving many **logistical** problems, such as finding reliable transportation and buying food for the trip.
   a. sensible
   b. educational
   c. organizational

9. The United Nations Children's Fund (UNICEF) has several **initiatives** that aim to protect and help children all over the world.
   a. offices where people work
   b. plans for achieving a purpose
   c. employees who work for an organization

10. It is easy for media companies to **transmit** ideas and information to the public via the Internet.
    a. look for or find
    b. send or broadcast
    c. see or read

11. It is difficult to deliver newspapers to people who live in **isolated** areas.
    a. far away; cut off from others
    b. large and crowded
    c. expensive and developed

12. Cell phones and MP3 players are examples of **devices** that are easy to carry and can store audio files.
    a. tools
    b. lies
    c. methods

PREVIEW LISTENING 2

Pod-Ready: Podcasting for the Developing World

You are going to listen to a podcast adapted from Scidev.Net, the website for the Science and Development Network, based in the United Kingdom. It examines both the popularity and the usefulness of podcasts.

Check (✓) the difficulties you think people in developing countries might have in getting news and information. Add your own ideas if you can.

☐ limited electricity   ☐ too much rain

☐ old equipment   ☐ limited education

☐ high cost   ☐ poor Internet access

☐ _____   ☐ _____

LISTEN FOR MAIN IDEAS

Level 9(CM)
Track 14

Listen to the podcast. Circle the correct answer.

1. Why are podcasts important to developing countries?
   a. They can provide a way for more people to get more information and different kinds of information.
   b. They are easier for people to understand than traditional forms of communication.
   c. They are more common there now than traditional forms of communication.

2. Why is radio less effective than podcasts?
   a. People in developing countries feel that radio is old-fashioned and that developed countries prefer podcasts.
   b. Radio needs a more reliable power source.
   c. Radio has less flexibility and is more expensive than podcasts.

3. What conclusion did McChesney draw from noticing that Peruvian people preferred the telephone to the computer?
   a. The people preferred to communicate and receive information through audio.
   b. More education and training would be needed before people could use computers well.
   c. Computers didn't provide access to the kind of information people wanted.

4. What is important about the e-tuk tuk in Sri Lanka?
   a. It provides a totally new way for people to stay connected with local, national, and international news.
   b. It uses modern technology to communicate in a traditional style.
   c. It proves that this kind of system can be used anywhere in the world.

5. What does David Benning believe about the future of podcasts in developing countries?
   a. The technology will remain limited because of basic access problems such as a poor electric power supply and the lack of special machines and parts.
   b. The technology will adapt to the special conditions and needs of developing countries.
   c. Developing countries will someday enjoy the same type of information and communication technology (ICT) as the developed world, but it may take another 10 or 15 years.

an e-tuk tuk

LISTEN FOR DETAILS

Level 9(CM)
Track 15

Read the statements. Then listen again. Write *T* (true) or *F* (false) according to what the speakers say. Then correct the false statements with a partner.

____ 1. ICT stands for International Communication Technology.

____ 2. Podcasts started in about 1994.

____ 3. It is more expensive to broadcast by radio than by podcasting.

____ 4. Local people in developing countries asked to be taught how to make podcasts.

_____ 5. Podcasting is popular because it is a one-way medium.

_____ 6. You need a license in order to create a podcast.

_____ 7. Most people in the Cajamarca region of Peru make a living through manufacturing.

_____ 8. Practical Action set up solar-powered computers in the Cajamarca region.

_____ 9. The residents of the Cajamarca region had Internet access for two hours a day.

_____ 10. The residents of the Cajamarca region want information that will help support their livelihoods.

_____ 11. The biggest barrier for podcasting to overcome is to find cheaper digital audio players.

_____ 12. In Zimbabwe, Practical Action is researching how to use podcasts to educate girls while they work.

WHAT DO YOU THINK?

A. Discuss the questions in a group.

1. Why do you think radios and telephones are the preferred devices for communication in many developing countries?

2. Do you agree or disagree that podcasts could become the solution to providing education in remote or isolated places?

3. What do you think is the biggest obstacle to overcome in order to help people get the news in developing countries? What is the best solution?

B. Think about both Listening 1 and Listening 2 as you discuss the questions.

1. What do you think influences people most in choosing a media format?

2. What changes do you predict we will see in the way people create and receive news and information over the next 50 years?

A **learner's dictionary** gives you more than just the definition and pronunciation of words. It also gives important information about each word that will help you use it correctly. You may find synonyms, antonyms, common expressions, and grammatical information.

The entry for *mainstream* shown below gives information about:

- **parts of speech:** It can be a singular noun, an adjective, and a verb.
- **meanings:** The most common meaning or use is listed first.
- **usage:** There are often notes, such as, for the adjective form, [*usually before noun*].
- **examples:** There are often example sentences, such as *Vegetarianism has been mainstreamed.*

---

main·stream /ˈmeɪnstrim/ *noun, adj., verb*
● **noun the mainstream** [sing.] the ideas and opinions that are thought to be normal because they are shared by most people; the people whose ideas and opinions are most accepted: *His radical views place him outside the mainstream of American politics.* ▶ **main·stream** *adj.* [usually before noun]: *mainstream education*

● **verb 1 ~ sth** to make a particular idea or opinion accepted by most people: *Vegetarianism has been mainstreamed.*
2 ~ sb to include children with mental or physical problems in ordinary school classes

---

The labels and abbreviations may not be the same in every dictionary. Check the front or back pages of the dictionary for a guide. Here are some common abbreviations.

adj.	adjective	**n.**	noun	**sth**	something
adv.	adverb	**pl.**	plural	**T**	transitive verb (verb followed by noun)
BrE	British English	**pt**	past tense	**U**	uncountable (another term for *noncount*)
C	countable noun	**sb**	somebody	**US**	American English
I	intransitive verb (verb not followed by noun)	**sing.**	singular	**v.**	verb

All dictionary entries are from the *Oxford Advanced American Dictionary for learners of English* © Oxford University Press 2011.

A. Work with a partner. Use a dictionary to find answers to these questions.

1. Which of these words is *not* both a noun and a verb: *network, inform, hurdle*?

    _____

2. What is the negative or opposite form of *finite*? _____

3. What preposition is used with *isolate*? _____ _____

4. What are two synonyms of *upfront*? _____

5. What is the noun form of *feasible*? _____

    Is it a countable or an uncountable noun? _____

6. What two adjectives are shown as commonly used with the noun *component*?

    _____

B. Circle the correct word or phrase to complete each sentence. Look up the
underlined words and phrase in a dictionary to check your answers.

1. Reporters are <u>accountable</u> (to / for) their readers and so they should check
   their facts carefully.

2. His blogs were outside (the <u>mainstream</u> / the <u>mainstreams</u>) of news media.

3. The story <u>compelled</u> him (to take / from taking) action.

4. To be left to your own (<u>devices</u> / <u>device</u>) means to be left alone without
   being told what to do.

5. <u>On demand</u> is a(n) (verb phrase / idiom).

6. <u>Prospect</u> is a(n) (uncountable / countable) noun when it means *possibility that
   something will happen*.

Reporters should check their facts.

SPEAKING

Often it is possible to create an adjective from a verb by using the present or past participle form of the verb.

Present participial adjectives

The **present participle** is the *-ing* form of a verb. A present participial adjective is used to describe:

- an ongoing state

You can get **breaking** news on the Internet. (The news is happening now.)

- the cause of a feeling or emotion

The students thought that TV news was **boring**. (TV news causes the feeling.)

Past participial adjectives

The **past participle** is the verb form used in perfect and passive sentences. The form is usually verb + *-ed*, but there are also several irregular verbs, such as *written* and *spoken*. A past participial adjective is used to describe:

- a completed state

Ben's iPod is **broken**; he has to borrow his friend's. (The iPod does not work.)

- the person or thing that feels or has the quality of the adjective

The students are **bored**. They don't have patience with TV news. (Students feel bored.)

Note: Past participial adjectives can only be formed from verbs that take an object (transitive verbs).

Note: You can form both present and past participial adjectives from some verbs. Use your dictionary if you are not sure.

In **developed** countries, there are many sources of news.
In **developing** countries, it can be difficult to get the news.

The past participial adjective *developed* refers to countries that are already advanced economically, while *developing* refers to those that are still developing their economies.

A. Read the sentences and circle the correct participial adjective.

1. The most (interesting / interested) news stories make the front page.

2. The editor told Louisa that her article was very well (writing / written).

3. Online weather websites have up-to-date information on (approaching / approached) storms.

4. The (downloading / downloaded) podcasts can be transferred to any audio device.

5. The bloggers who publish the most (compelling / compelled) stories become famous.

6. An (illustrated / illustrating) story is easier for young readers to understand.

B. Work with a partner. Write a short conversation about new media. One partner talks about its advantages, and one partner talks about its disadvantages. Use at least three present and three past participial adjectives in the conversation. Create adjectives from the verbs in the box, or choose your own. Practice your conversation and then present it to the class.

bore	develop	frustrate	surprise
compel	excite	interest	tire

A: *What are you listening to?*
B: *It's a really exciting podcast about the election. Want to hear it?*
A: *No, thanks. I'm not very interested.*
B: *Don't you think the election is interesting?*
A: *I do, but podcasts are so boring. I'd rather read the newspaper.*

There are only five letters that represent vowels (*a, e, i, o, u*), but there are 15 vowel sounds. They may sound similar, but failure to produce them correctly or distinguish between them can lead to misunderstanding. As an example, the letter *a* can be pronounced as /æ/ in *hat*, /ɑ/ in *father*, or /eɪ/ in *relate*.

Vowel sounds change with slight variations in your mouth (the shape of your lips and the positions of your tongue and jaw). Pay attention to how your mouth changes as you make these sounds one after another:

- /eɪ/ Your tongue should be in the front and middle of your mouth with your jaw slightly open and your lips spread.
- /æ/ Your tongue moves lower, your jaw opens a little wider, and your lips spread more.
- /ɑ/ Your tongue is lowest in your mouth as your jaw opens widest and your lips open wide as if you are yawning.
- /oʊ/ Your tongue shifts back in your mouth as your jaw starts to close and your lips are rounded.

A common rule is that when *a* and *o* are the only vowels in a one-syllable word, *a* is often pronounced /æ/ as in *hat* and *o* is pronounced /ɑ/ as in *not*. However, when a final *-e* is added, they are usually pronounced as /eɪ/ and /oʊ/ as in *hate* and *note*.

Level 9(CM)
Track 16

Listen and repeat the examples in the chart. Pay attention to the way your mouth changes.

/eɪ/	/æ/	/ɑ/	/oʊ/
stake	stack	stock	stroke
late	land	lot	lone
made	mad	mod	mode
plane	plan	plod	explode
rate	rat	rot	remote

It is also important to remember that all vowels in an unstressed syllable can be reduced to the schwa /ə/ sound. The first unstressed syllables in *about* and *concede* are pronounced as /ə/.

A. Work with a partner. Read the paragraphs about the ideas in Listening 1 and Listening 2 out loud. Pay special attention to the underlined parts of the bold words.

1. Robin Hamman works for Headshift, which is an **agency** that advises **organizations** and governments on **blogging** and other **aspects** of **social** media. He **states** that often citizen journalists are **common** people who work **alone** and just **happen** to have **access** at the **moment** a story breaks. There are many **examples** of such **accidental** journalists who then **create documents** on their computers and **upload** them to a website. He thinks journalists with a bias should be **honest**, but **also** need to **watch** out to make sure their opinions **don't** affect the coverage of the story.

2. Ben McChesney works for **Practical** Action, a charity group that **hopes** to bring **technology** to poor rural areas so farmers can produce **podcasts**. What **makes** podcasting more **attractive** than **radio** is its **low** cost. On one **project** in Peru, McChesney realized the **telephone** was more **popular** than the computer. People preferred audio to text for some **information**. His group is working **on** new ways to **promote** education through podcasts.

 Level 9(CM)
Track 17

B. Listen to the excerpts from Activity A and check your pronunciation. Then write each bold word from Activity A in the correct place in the chart according to the pronunciation of the underlined syllable. Compare your chart with a partner.

/eɪ/	/æ/	/ɑ/	/oʊ/
agency			

C. Work with a partner. Ask and answer the questions.

1. What are some advantages of blogging?

2. What are some advantages of self-produced podcasts?

3. What do blogs and podcasts have in common?

It is important to be organized when you give presentations. Note cards are a simple way to make sure you say everything you want to say, in the correct order. Note cards act as reminders; they should not be a complete transcript of your talk!

Here are some tips for preparing effective note cards.

- Use index cards. Plan to use one or two cards per minute of speaking.
- Write key words from the main ideas you plan to speak about in big, clear letters on one side.
- List examples or details (using numbers or bullets) on the other side.
- Don't write complete sentences.
- Make your words large enough to see easily.
- Number your cards in case they fall out of order.

Here are some tips for speaking with note cards.

- Practice a few times in front of a mirror or a friend before you speak to a group.
- Try to look at your cards less and less each time you speak.
- Remember not to speak too fast or read your note cards.
- Look at your audience most of the time; only look at each note card briefly as necessary.

Here is an example of one student's note card, front and back.

Tip for Success

PowerPoint slides are like note cards, but your audience can see them, too. Turn your key words into headings and make a bulleted list on each slide to help you and your audience stay focused through a speech.

1

podcast definition

- digital audio file
- downloaded from the Internet to computer
- can be put on MP3 player
- iPods

Here is what the student might say from this note card during a speech.

> Many of you probably already know what a podcast is. But just to be clear and accurate, a podcast is a digital audio file that is downloaded from the Internet onto your computer. Then, you can transfer it to an mp3 player, like an iPod. In fact, the word *podcast* comes from the brand name iPod.

A. Choose three of the topics below. Write each topic on the back of a note card. Then complete your note cards with your own ideas. (If you do not have note cards, do the work in your notebook.)

my media preferences	podcasting: pros or cons
different types of media	popularity of social networking sites
where to go for online news	types of "citizen media"
how to write a blog	problems with today's media

There are many ways to get the news today.

B. Work with a partner. Present a 1–2 minute talk each on one aspect of new media. Use your note cards as necessary. When you have both finished, change partners and repeat the exercise. Did you use your note cards less the second time?

In this section, you will survey people about their media preferences. As you prepare your survey and discuss the results, think about the Unit Question, "How do people get the news today?" and refer to the Self-Assessment checklist on page 50.

For alternative unit assignments, see the *Q: Skills for Success Teacher's Handbook*.

CONSIDER THE IDEAS

Work in a group. Look at the photo. Then discuss the questions below.

1. How are the man and woman in this photo accessing news and information?

2. What types of media do you think your classmates use to get news and information? Do you think they are similar to the man in the photo or the woman?

PREPARE AND SPEAK

A. **GATHER IDEAS** Work in a group. Complete the tasks below to create and conduct a survey about news habits in your classroom or community.

1. Brainstorm a list of *Yes / No* questions about where, how, and how often people get their news.

2. Practice asking your questions to your group members and brainstorm possible follow-up questions together.

3. Each group member should choose 6–8 questions. You do *not* all need to choose the same ones! Then create a chart like the one below to write questions and record responses.

Question	Yes	No	Further Information
Do you ever listen to the news on Internet radio?	☐	☑	already listens to news on car radio while driving to school
Are blogs more useful than books for keeping up with the news?	☑	☐	information is more current

4. Each group member should survey ten people outside of class if possible (if necessary, you can speak to classmates). You will need to complete one survey form for each person you interview or create a chart large enough to record the information from ten people.

B. **ORGANIZE IDEAS** Follow these steps to analyze the information from your survey. (Note that the small sample size of ten people means that your "statistics" are not accurate for a general population! You are practicing with the language of reporting surveys.)

1. Tally your answers; that is, how many people answered each question *yes* or *no*? Circle any interesting extra information that you might want to use in your talk.

2. Write the percentages of *yes* answers and *no* answers on your chart. For example, if four people said they listen to the news on Internet radio, then write the figure 40%.

3. Decide which questions gave you the most interesting or important information. You may choose to speak about only a few questions, or you could speak about all of them.

4. Prepare note cards for your presentation.

C. **SPEAK** Present the results of your survey to your group or the whole class. Remember to summarize detailed information with main ideas. Start with an overall main idea for your group report. Each speaker should use note cards, but only as a guide. Refer to the Self-Assessment checklist below before you begin.

CHECK AND REFLECT

A. **CHECK** Think about the Unit Assignment as you complete the Self-Assessment checklist.

Yes	No	SELF-ASSESSMENT
☐	☐	I was able to speak fluently about the topic.
☐	☐	My group or class understood me.
☐	☐	I used both main ideas and details.
☐	☐	I used participial adjectives correctly.
☐	☐	I used vocabulary from the unit to express my ideas.
☐	☐	I pronounced vowels correctly.
☐	☐	I used note cards to communicate more effectively.

B. **REFLECT** Discuss these questions with a partner.

What is something new you learned in this unit?

 Look back at the Unit Question. Is your answer different now than when you started this unit? If yes, how is it different? Why?

Circle the words and phrase you learned in this unit.

Nouns
bias AWL
component 🔑 AWL
device 🔑 AWL
foundation 🔑 AWL
initiative 🔑 AWL
medium 🔑 AWL
networking AWL
source 🔑 AWL
technique 🔑 AWL
viewpoint

Verbs
transmit AWL
unfold

Adjectives
accidental 🔑
accountable
anonymous
compelling
feasible
finite AWL
isolated AWL

liberating AWL
logistical
unique 🔑 AWL
upfront

Phrase
on demand (idiom)

🔑 Oxford 3000™ words
AWL Academic Word List

Check (✓) the skills you learned. If you need more work on a skill, refer to the page(s) in parentheses.

LISTENING ●	I can identify main ideas. (p. 33)
VOCABULARY ●	I can understand a dictionary entry. (p. 40)
GRAMMAR ●	I can understand and use participial adjectives. (p. 42)
PRONUNCIATION ●	I can correctly pronounce the vowels *a* and *o*. (p. 44)
SPEAKING ●	I can use note cards effectively when I speak. (p. 46)
LEARNING OUTCOME ●	I can develop and administer a survey focused on media preferences, analyze the results, and report my findings.

UNIT 3	Language		
	LISTENING	●	making inferences
	VOCABULARY	●	negative prefixes
	GRAMMAR	●	passive voice
	PRONUNCIATION	●	emphatic word stress
	SPEAKING	●	using figurative language

FRANCE

Develop a narrative incorporating figurative language that chronologically details an incident of language loss or an inability to communicate.

Unit QUESTION

How does language affect who we are?

PREVIEW THE UNIT

(A) Discuss these questions with your classmates.

What difficulties might an English speaker visiting your home country have while trying to communicate?

Do people who know two languages have different thoughts in each language or just different words for them?

Look at the photo. How are the people communicating? What are other forms of non-standard communication?

(B) Discuss the Unit Question above with your classmates.

Listen to Level 9(CM), Track 18 to hear other answers.

C Work with a partner. Read the following situations and discuss them. Then choose one and role-play it for the class.

Have you ever experienced one of these difficulties in communicating?

1. Two friends see each other across a large, crowded, noisy restaurant. They try to communicate different issues, such as the time (one person is late), where to sit, and whether or not to leave.

2. A tourist who doesn't speak the language is lost in a big city. He or she tries to get directions from a local resident to get to a specific location (such as a hospital, a train station, a restaurant, or a museum).

3. A patient in a doctor's office tries to explain to the doctor how he or she woke up with a terrible headache and weak muscles and now is unable to speak.

Tip Critical Thinking

In Activity D, you will **give examples** of the different kinds of causes and effects. Giving examples shows you understand concepts.

D With your partner, use this mind map to brainstorm causes and effects of communication difficulties such as those in Activity C or another situation. Then discuss the questions below using your mind map.

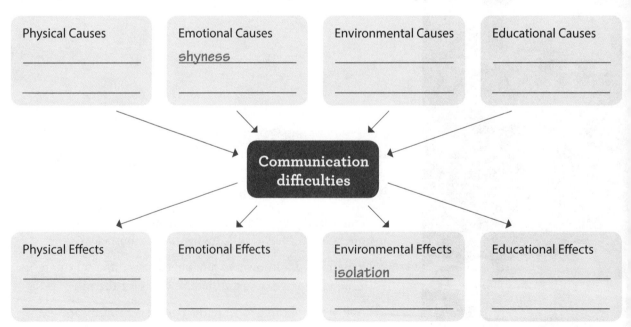

Physical Causes	Emotional Causes	Environmental Causes	Educational Causes
_____	_shyness_	_____	_____
_____	_____	_____	_____

Communication difficulties

Physical Effects	Emotional Effects	Environmental Effects	Educational Effects
_____	_____	_isolation_	_____
_____	_____	_____	_____

1. What do you think are the most common causes?

2. What are the most harmful effects?

LISTENING 1 | My Stroke of Insight: A Brain Scientist's Personal Journey

VOCABULARY

Here are some words from Listening 1. Read the paragraphs. Then write each bold word next to the correct definition.

The brain is one of the most **fascinating** organs in the human body, partly because it is such a mystery. It is studied by doctors called neurologists and neuroanatomists, who hope to gain an **insight** into the way the brain works. The **structure** of the brain is important: it is divided into two equal sections called hemispheres. One part, the cerebral cortex, coordinates what we think and feel with what we see and our **perceptions** of the outside world. Each part of the brain has a specific **function**, and if injured, it may become unable to perform this role.

1. _____ *(n.)* awareness; how things are noticed by the senses

2. _____ *(n.)* an understanding of what something is like

3. _____ *(adj.)* extremely interesting

4. _____ *(n.)* the purpose of someone or something

5. _____ *(n.)* the way in which the parts of something are arranged or organized

A stroke occurs when blood flow to part of the brain is cut off due to a hemorrhage (heavy bleeding); this can result in an inability to speak or move. Stroke victims sometimes lose **consciousness** and later have no memory of what has happened. They may not be aware of **external** events or things around them. The line between what is real and unreal may become unclear, and the inability to understand this **boundary** may cause confusion. However, some patients experience the opposite feeling of **tranquil** euphoria, a sense of calm when they are disconnected from the real world. For all stroke victims, **recovery** depends on the seriousness of the stroke, but with a lot of physical and speech therapy, patients can **regain** their ability to walk and communicate. Although the **overall** survival rate for stroke victims is not bad, on the whole, 40 percent have some resulting disability.

6. _____ *(v.)* get back something you no longer have, especially an ability or quality

7. _____ *(n.)* the state of being aware of something

8. _____ (n.) the process of becoming well again after an illness or an injury

9. _____ (adj.) quiet; peaceful

10. _____ (adj.) happening or coming from outside a place or your situation

11. _____ (adj.) general; considering everything

12. _____ (n.) a real or imaginary border; a dividing line

PREVIEW LISTENING 1

Dr. Jill Bolte Taylor

My Stroke of Insight: A Brain Scientist's Personal Journey

You are going to listen to a radio interview. Dr. Jill Bolte Taylor is a neuroanatomist who had a stroke and later wrote a book titled *My Stroke of Insight: A Brain Scientist's Story*. She describes the effects of her stroke in her book and in this interview with David Inge of radio station WILL from the University of Illinois.

How do you think Dr. Taylor's ability to think and communicate was affected when she had a stroke? Check (✓) your prediction.

☐ She could think using language, but could not speak.

☐ She could not think or speak using language.

LISTEN FOR MAIN IDEAS

 Level 9(CM)
Track 19

A. Read the key phrases in the chart that indicate main ideas. Listen to the interview and take notes to explain the ideas.

 Tip for Success

Anticipating key words or phrases about a topic, and then taking notes about them when you listen, will help you understand and remember the details.

Introduction

Key Phrases	Notes
1. The right hemisphere and the big picture	
2. The left hemisphere and language	

Call-in Show

Key Phrases	Notes
3. Memories and a sense of identity	
4. Stroke victims and English speakers in a foreign country	

B. Use your notes to write the main ideas that Taylor explains to her listeners. Compare your sentences with a partner.

Introduction

1. The right hemisphere and the big picture

   _____

   _____

2. The left hemisphere and language

   _____

   _____

Call-in Show

3. Memories and a sense of identity

   _____

   _____

4. Stroke victims and English speakers in a foreign country

   _____

   _____

LISTEN FOR DETAILS

 Level 9(CM)
Track 20

Listen again. Circle the answer that best completes each statement.

Introduction

1. When Jill Bolte Taylor had her stroke in 1996, she was working at (Harvard / Indiana) University.

2. Dr. Taylor describes her feeling during her stroke as one of (peace and tranquility / panic and fear).

3. The two halves of the brain process information in (similar / different) ways.

4. The right hemisphere of the brain is concerned with (overall perception / details).

5. The right and left hemispheres (have to / don't have to) work together for people to have a normal perspective.

6. When Dr. Taylor had a stroke, she lost the (right / left) hemisphere of her brain.

Call-in Show

7. The behavioral psychologists mentioned by the caller believed that language could be lost only if a person (remained conscious / lost consciousness).

8. Dr. Taylor lost her perception of (past and present / past and future).

9. According to Taylor, a tourist who doesn't speak the language will have (less / greater) awareness of other communicative signals, such as people's voices and facial expressions.

10. When Dr. Taylor lost the basic human ability to use language, she (no longer saw herself / still saw herself) as a human being.

 WHAT DO YOU THINK?

Discuss the questions in a group.

1. Do you think you focus more on "the big picture" and general ideas or details? Would you say that you are more "right-brained" or "left-brained," according to the ideas in the Listening?

2. Which effect of a stroke would upset you more, the loss of the ability to speak or the loss of your past memories? Why?

3. Describe your overall perception of one of the pictures, which will engage the right hemisphere of your brain (the side that looks at the big picture). Describe the details of the other picture, which will engage the left hemisphere of your brain (the side that looks at details).

Picture A

Picture B

Listening Skill | Making inferences

Speakers do not always state their ideas or opinions directly. They may give facts or examples and expect the listener to draw a logical conclusion, or *make an inference*. It is important, however, to make sure you don't make inferences that were not suggested by the information!

If you are not sure what someone is implying, here are some phrases to check your understanding.

> So, do you mean that . . . ?
> So, are you saying that . . . ?
> So, would you say that . . . ?

 Track 9 (CM)
Track 21

A. Listen to the excerpts from Listening 1. Circle the best inference for each one.

1. a. People have no idea how the brain works.
   b. People don't understand the exact functions of the different parts of the brain.

2. a. A normal, healthy person uses both hemispheres.
   b. Different people prefer to use different hemispheres of the brain.

3. a. Dr. Taylor found an advantage in the results of her stroke.
   b. Dr. Taylor was very upset at losing some of her brain's abilities.

4. a. Dr. Taylor feels that foreign tourists function somewhat as if they were brain-damaged.

   b. Dr. Taylor feels that foreign tourists make up for the lack of language skills by increasing other communicative abilities.

B. Choose two of the situations below or use your own ideas. Write some sentences that imply the ideas—but do not state them directly!

Your concerns about learning English
Your communication difficulties with grandparents
Your thoughts on teenage slang and text abbreviations
Your feelings about your language classes
Your fears about a miscommunication with a best friend

Your idea: _____

Your idea: _____

C. Work with a partner. Take turns reading the sentences about your situation. Can your partner infer what you are trying to say?

LISTENING 2 | The Story of My Life

VOCABULARY

Here are some words from Listening 2. Read the sentences. Circle the answer that best matches the meaning of each bold word.

1. Children learn to speak by **imitating** words and trying to sound like adults.
   a. copying   b. ignoring

2. When we were trying to use our hands to communicate without language, we found that the way we **gesticulated** did not always get the message across.
   a. made signs with our hands   b. complained loudly

3. There were many **incidents** that showed the child's frustration with learning the language, even though she never said anything directly.
   a. results   b. examples

4. The experience was so **intense** that it caused the woman to cry.
   a. powerful
   b. unexpected

5. If you feel your language skills are **adequate** for that job, then you should apply!
   a. good enough
   b. not good enough

6. Those who are bilingual **invariably** get jobs more easily and are grateful to their parents for making them learn a second language.
   a. almost never
   b. almost always

7. These passionate **outbursts** helped the little boy get his way because no one could ignore the noise he made.
   a. sudden strong expressions of emotion
   b. songs

8. Without **tangible** evidence to support their theory, the researchers didn't feel confident publishing their study.
   a. popular; widely accepted
   b. clearly seen to exist; able to be touched

9. The answer to the mystery was not **revealed** until the last few pages of the book.
   a. explained; shown
   b. hidden

10. If that annoying sound **persists**, I will have to complain to the neighbors. I can't sleep!
    a. gets louder
    b. continues

11. Because the stroke victim had lost some of her vision, she could only make out **fragments** of the picture and had to connect the pieces in her mind.
    a. small portions; bits
    b. soft colors

12. There was no strong **sentiment** visible in the actor's face, no feeling of anger or sorrow.
    a. damaged area
    b. emotion

Annie Sullivan and Helen Keller

PREVIEW LISTENING 2

The Story of My Life

You are going to listen to an excerpt from an audiobook of Hellen Keller's autobiography, *The Story of My Life*. Helen Keller (1880–1968) lost her sight and her hearing from an illness when she was 19 months old. She learned to communicate through hard work with her teacher, Annie Sullivan.

In what ways do you predict a child who lost her sight and hearing at such a young age would try to communicate? Write your ideas.

_____

_____

_____

_____

LISTEN FOR MAIN IDEAS

Level 9(CM)
Track 22

Read the descriptions of Helen Keller's emotions during each period of her life. Then listen to the audiobook excerpt. Write the letter of the description under the event on the timeline on page 63. Compare your answers with a partner.

a. Helen could make finger signs to spell many words but became <u>impatient</u> because she didn't understand how the actions connected with the words.

b. Helen used her hands, touched every object, and felt <u>protected</u> by her mother who understood her crude signs to communicate.

c. Helen's desire to communicate grew so strong that she was often <u>angry</u> and had passionate outbursts.

d. Helen grew <u>confident</u> as she explored with her hands and learned the names and uses for objects.

e. Helen understood what was going on about her and could imitate actions, but she felt <u>different</u> from others.

f. Helen touched people's lips and imitated their movements but became <u>frustrated</u> when it did not produce any result.

g. Helen felt <u>free and hopeful</u> once the mystery of language was revealed to her, and she was <u>eager</u> to learn.

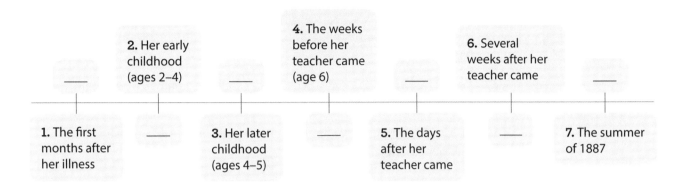

Helen Keller's Life

2. Her early childhood (ages 2–4) ____

4. The weeks before her teacher came (age 6) ____

6. Several weeks after her teacher came ____

1. The first months after her illness ____

3. Her later childhood (ages 4–5) ____

5. The days after her teacher came ____

7. The summer of 1887

LISTEN FOR DETAILS

 Level 9(CM)
Track 23

Read the lists of examples and descriptions from the audiobook excerpt. Then listen again. Match the examples with the descriptions.

 Tip for Success

Over time, the meaning of a word can change. The word *dumb*, for example, means "unable to speak," but today the meaning "unintelligent" is more common. Check up-to-date dictionaries and ask your teacher if you are confused about a word.

a. touching with her hands

b. a doll

c. pushing someone to tell her to go

d. her teacher

e. the strength of the sun

f. water

g. her mother

h. breaking the doll

i. touching someone's lips and trying to move her own

j. knowing which clothes meant she was going out

____ 1. an example of Helen's simple "crude signs" to communicate

____ 2. the person to whom Helen owed "all that was bright and good in my long night"

____ 3. Helen's saying "She brought me my hat, and I knew I was going out" is an example of Helen's understanding of what was going on about her

____ 4. the way Helen tried to learn to speak that left her "so angry at times that [she] kicked and screamed until [she] was exhausted"

_____ 5. the person "who had come to reveal all things to me, and, more than all things else, to love me"

_____ 6. the way Helen knew that the "sweet southern spring" season had begun

_____ 7. the gift that "the little blind children at the Perkins Institution had sent"

_____ 8. the "living word" that "awakened [her] soul" and made Helen finally realize what language was

_____ 9. the action that Helen said made her feel satisfied and showed she knew "neither sorrow nor regret"

_____ 10. the way Helen explored her world in order to "learn the name of every object"

WHAT DO YOU THINK?

A. Discuss the questions in a group.

1. In the modern world, do you think it is better for a child like Helen Keller to have a private tutor at home or learn in a school setting?

2. Helen Keller felt lost and empty without language. She was angry and even violent at times when she couldn't communicate. What are some emotions that are hard to put into words, and how do different people express them?

3. What message do you think Helen Keller wants readers to get from her descriptions of her childhood before and after she met her teacher?

B. Think about both Listening 1 and Listening 2 as you discuss the questions.

1. If Helen Keller and Jill Bolte Taylor could meet, what do you think they would talk about?

2. What mental attitudes did Helen Keller and Jill Bolte Taylor have in common? In what ways were their attitudes different?

Knowledge of prefixes helps you expand your vocabulary. Here are prefixes that are added to adjectives to give an opposite or negative meaning.

il-   **il**legal
im-   **im**possible
in-   **in**capable
ir-   **ir**regular
un-   **un**thinkable

Tip for Success

Although we rarely stress prefixes, we put strong secondary stress on a prefix that means *not* so it is easy for a listener to understand the negative meaning (<u>un</u>imPORtant, <u>dys</u>FUNCtional).

With *il-*, *im-*, and *ir-*, there are patterns, but also exceptions.

Use *il-* for words that begin with *l*.	**il**legal, **il**logical (but **un**lawful)
Use *im-* for words that begin with *p*, *m*, and *b*.	**im**possible, **im**measurable (but **un**popular)
Use *ir-* for words that begin with *r*.	**ir**relevant, **ir**regular (but **un**reliable)

The prefix *dis-* is the form that is most often used to form the negative of verbs, though *un-* is also used.

disagree   **dis**obey   **dis**qualify   **dis**like   **un**do   **un**tie

Both *dis-* and *un-* are also used for participial adjectives.

dissatisfied   **dis**appointing   **un**decided   **un**ending

A. Write the correct negative prefix on the line in front of the adjectives.

1. Dr. Taylor said that she was able to enjoy the experience of being
   ____connected from the left hemisphere of her brain.

2. Dr. Taylor told the caller she wasn't ____conscious even though she
   had had a stroke.

3. The caller was surprised that the neuroanatomist could get help in
   spite of her ____regular style of communicating.

4. A stroke victim who wasn't a doctor like Taylor was could have been
   ____aware of what was happening.

5. Helen Keller's parents might have thought that a teacher without direct experience with blindness would have been more ____sensitive about Helen's condition.

6. Helen Keller was ____patient with her teacher's attempts to teach her the difference between *mug* and *water*.

B. Write sentences to describe Helen Keller and Jill Bolte Taylor. Use one of these adjectives in a negative form in each sentence. Compare sentences with a partner.

adequate	conscious	perfect	tangible
capable	connected	possible	usual
comfortable	measurable	satisfied	visible

Helen Keller's earliest attempts to communicate were inadequate.

1. _____

_____

2. _____

_____

3. _____

_____

4. _____

_____

from the movie *The Miracle Worker*

Grammar   Passive voice

1. The **passive voice** is used to put the emphasis on the object of the verb instead of the subject.

For example, imagine we want to talk about why Jill Bolte Taylor lost her language ability: because of the effects of a stroke on her brain. The most important part of the sentence is *her brain* and not a *stroke*. Therefore, instead of the active sentence *A stroke damaged Taylor's brain* we would say:

☐   Taylor's brain **was damaged** by a stroke.

2. The passive voice is used when the subject of the sentence isn't known.

☐   This audiobook **was recorded** in 2007.

If we don't know (and don't care) who recorded the audiobook, it sounds awkward to say *Somebody recorded this audio book in 2007*. The important element of the sentence is *this audiobook*, so it sounds better at the beginning of the sentence.

3. The passive voice is only used with **transitive verbs** (verbs that take an object).

   ✓   Helen Keller **was taught** a new way to speak.

   ✗   Dr. Taylor's stroke was happened in the morning.

4. In passive sentences, the verb tense is indicated in the verb *be*. Modal verbs can also be made passive.

Past perfect passive	Past passive	Present perfect passive
had been found	was lost	has been studied
Present passive	**Future passive**	**Modal passive**
is taken	will be given	may be revealed could be gained

The active voice is more common than the passive voice. Overusing the passive voice can make your speaking sound flat, impersonal, or too formal. This is why some word-processing grammar checks underline passive sentences. However, there are times when the passive voice is more appropriate and should be used.

Tip for Success

Remember that not all sentences with a form of *be* + a participle are passive! *This article was written by Helen Keller* is passive. *I was tired after a long, difficult day* is not passive. It is the simple past of the verb *be* + an adjective.

A. Read these sentences from Helen Keller's story. Write *P* if the underlined verb is passive and *A* if it is active.

_____ 1. I felt my teacher sweep the fragments to one side of the hearth, and I had a sense of satisfaction that the cause of my discomfort <u>was removed</u>.

_____ 2. She brought me my hat, and I knew I <u>was going out</u> into the warm sunshine.

_____ 3. This thought, if a wordless sensation <u>may be called</u> a thought, made me hop and skip with pleasure.

_____ 4. Someone <u>was drawing</u> water, and my teacher placed my hand under the spout.

_____ 5. As the cool stream gushed over one hand she <u>spelled</u> into the other the word *water*, first slowly, then rapidly.

_____ 6. I stood still; my whole attention <u>was fixed</u> upon the motions of her fingers.

_____ 7. Suddenly I felt a misty consciousness as of something that <u>had been forgotten</u>—a thrill of returning thought; and somehow the mystery of language was revealed to me.

_____ 8. I knew then that "w-a-t-e-r" meant the wonderful cool something that <u>was flowing</u> over my hand.

B. Work with a partner. Discuss whether the passive or the active version of the sentence sounds more natural. (Sometimes one is clearly better; sometimes both can sound all right, although the emphasis is different.)

1. a. I forgot my textbook.
   b. My textbook was forgotten by me.

2. a. Some scientists made many significant advances in the field of neuroscience in the last century.
   b. Many significant advances in the field of neuroscience were made in the last century.

3. a. Louis Braille invented a system of writing for the blind known as Braille.
   b. Braille, a system of writing for the blind, was invented by Louis Braille.

4. a. Someone added Braille signs to places such as elevators and restrooms.
   b. Braille signs have been added to places such as elevators and restrooms.

5. a. Today, some blind children may attend regular public schools.

   b. Today, regular public schools may be attended by some blind children.

6. a. Helen Keller's story inspired me.

   b. I was inspired by Helen Keller's story.

Pronunciation   Emphatic word stress

Speakers engage their audiences by emphasizing key words in three main ways.

1. Saying key words more loudly
2. Making the vowels in the key syllables longer
3. Using a higher pitch for stressed words

Key words in sentences are usually content words (nouns, verbs, adjectives, and adverbs).

We also stress words that provide new information or information that contrasts with or corrects previous information. New or particularly important information often comes at the end of a clause or sentence.

Level 9(CM)
Track 24

Listen and practice the examples.

> She's a SCIENTIST. (noun)
> She was COMPLETELY CONSCIOUS. (adverb + adjective)
> He was RESPONSIBLE. (adjective)
> She ISOLATED herself. (verb)

Any word (pronouns, auxiliaries, prepositions) can be stressed, however, when the speaker wants to emphasize a particular point. Notice which words indicate corrective or contrasting information.

Level 9(CM)
Track 24

Listen and practice the examples.

> A: She's a SCIENTIST?   B: No, she's a DENTIST.
> A: Are you afraid of oral reports?   B: YES! I NEVER take speaking classes.
> A: Can Gary speak MANDARIN?   B. HE can't, but LISA can.

When you emphasize key words, a strong rhythm develops and key words stand out clearly to listeners. Knowing how stress and intonation work will help you with both speaking fluency and listening comprehension.

A. Jill Bolte Taylor is a strong and dynamic speaker. Listen to her describe the morning of her stroke. Circle the key words you hear emphasized; then compare transcripts with a partner and discuss the ways the speaker uses stress to help tell her story.

Then I would have this wave of clarity that would bring me and reattach me back to normal reality, and I could pursue my plan, and my—the only plan that I had in my head was to call work and that somebody at work would get me help. Um, but it—it took, uh, over 45 minutes for me to figure out what number to dial and how to dial and by the time, um, I got the information I could not see uh the, the phone number on my business card. I couldn't pick the numbers out from the background pixels, cause all I could see were pixels. Uh, and it's a you know, it's a, big drama. By the time my colleague, I'm very fortunate he was at his desk. I spoke. I said "Woo Woo Woo Woo Er" I had no, no language and when he spoke to me he sounded "Woo Woo Wer." He sounded like a golden retriever. So, uh, but he did recognize that it was I and that I needed help and then eventually he did get me help.

B. In a group, take turns adding some expressive details to these sentence starters, stressing key words so your listeners understand what information is important or contrastive.

1. We use our right brains to . . . , and our left brains to . . . .

2. Many ESL learners have difficulty . . . , but I . . . .

3. When I had to stand up in front of the class to give a speech, ...

4. I'll never forget the day when (name of a person) asked me . . . .

5. When I went to visit my relatives in . . . , I couldn't . . . .

6. Taylor's experience made me think about . . . .

7. My worst experience trying to speak English was when . . . .

| Speaking Skill | Using figurative language |

One way to make your speaking more interesting is to use *similes* and *metaphors*. These devices create images that help listeners experience the intensity of something you are describing.

A **simile** is a way of describing something by comparing it to another thing. Similes include the word *like* or *as*.

> Learning English is **like** climbing a mountain.
> Her skin was as soft **as** silk.

Some similes become so common in a language that they become idioms.

> as pretty as a picture   as gentle as a lamb
> as sharp as a tack   roar like a lion

A **metaphor** describes something as if it were something else. Here, *words* are being compared to *swords that cut through the silence*.

> His **words** were swords that cut through the silence.

Metaphors can be quite indirect. Here, *his heart* is being described as if it were something that could actually *break*, such as glass.

> His **heart** was broken.

A. Match the parts of the phrases to form common similes in English.

____ 1. You are as light as   a. a baby

____ 2. That horse can run like   b. a bee

____ 3. When I lost my diamond ring, I cried like   c. a feather

____ 4. You are as busy as   d. a fish

____ 5. His words cut me like   e. a knife

____ 6. Please be as quiet as   f. a mouse

____ 7. The children were as good as   g. gold

____ 8. My sister can swim like   h. the wind

B. Work with a partner. Explain what the underlined metaphors from Listening 1 and Listening 2 mean. What is the literal meaning of the words?

1. These are all the memories associated with who I had been, and when that person went <u>offline</u>, which is the best way for me to explain it, I lost all of her likes and dislikes.

2. You wake up one day and you're in <u>the heart</u> of China.

3. That <u>living</u> word awakened my soul.

4. There were barriers still, it is true, but barriers that could in time be <u>swept</u> away.

5. . . . words that were to make the world <u>blossom</u> for me.

C. Work with a partner. Describe one of the items or situations below in a short paragraph. Use your imagination and be colorful! Use similes and metaphors. Then read your description to the class.

My room is a disaster area. It looks like a tornado blew through, scattering my papers like leaves in an autumn wind. If you can wade through the piles of clothes near my bed, . . .

1. Your room or home

2. Your friend or someone you know

3. Learning a new language

4. Speaking in front of the class

5. Being a tourist in a foreign country

6. Listening to music

Unit Assignment | **Narrate a personal experience**

 In this section, you will narrate an experience involving language loss or an inability to communicate. As you prepare your narrative, think about the Unit Question, "How does language affect who we are?" and refer to the Self-Assessment checklist on page 74.

For alternative unit assignments, see the *Q: Skills for Success Teacher's Handbook.*

CONSIDER THE IDEAS

A. Maxine Hong Kingston, a Chinese-American writer, was born in the United States, but her parents spoke only Chinese at home. In her autobiographical novel, *The Woman Warrior*, she describes her discomfort speaking English after years of silence in American school and narrates a painful experience in Chinese school. Read this excerpt.

When I went to kindergarten and had to speak English for the first time, I became silent. A dumbness—a shame—still cracks my voice in two, even when I want to say "hello" casually, or ask an easy question in front of the check-out counter, or ask directions of a bus driver. I stand frozen, or I hold up the line with the complete, grammatical sentence that comes squeaking out at impossible length. "What did you say?" says the cab driver, or "Speak up," so I have to perform again, only weaker the second time. A telephone call makes my throat bleed and takes up that day's courage. . . .

Not all of the children who were silent at American school found voice at Chinese school. One new teacher said each of us had to get up and recite in front of the class, who was to listen. My sister and I had memorized the lesson perfectly. We said it to each other at home, one chanting, one listening. The teacher called on my sister to recite first. It was the first time a teacher had called on the second-born to go first. My sister was scared. She glanced at me and looked away; I looked down at my desk. I hoped that she could do it because if she could, then I wouldn't have to. She opened her mouth and a voice came out that wasn't a whisper, but it wasn't a proper voice either. I hoped that she would not cry, fear breaking up her voice like twigs underfoot. She sounded as if she were trying to sing though weeping and strangling. She did not pause or stop to end the embarrassment. She kept going until she said the last word, and then she sat down. When it was my turn, the same voice came out, a crippled animal running on broken legs. You could hear splinters in my voice, bones rubbing jagged against one another. I was loud, though. I was glad I didn't whisper.

B. Discuss these questions with a group.

1. How did Hong Kingston's communication difficulties affect her identity?

2. In what ways can you relate to Hong Kingston's story about language and silence?

3. Discuss the similes and metaphors she uses. Which ones affected you the most?

PREPARE AND SPEAK

A. GATHER IDEAS Work in a group. Follow these steps to gather ideas.

1. Brainstorm examples of stories about language-related difficulties that you can use as models or inspiration for your narrative.

2. Talk about the stories you have listened to and read in this unit and the examples your classmates have shared. What makes these stories compelling?

3. When you have chosen an idea, briefly describe it to your group. Ask your group where they think your story should begin and end. Should you use a humorous or a serious tone?

B. ORGANIZE IDEAS Follow these steps to prepare your narrative.

1. Use a timeline like the one on page 63 to organize the main events and/ or emotional states in your story. Choose your starting and ending points. Make sure the emotions and events between are in chronological order.

2. Work with a partner. Practice narrating your stories to each other. Use your skills to make your story come alive.
   - metaphors and similes
   - positive and negative descriptive adjectives
   - emphasis on key words when speaking
   - hand gestures, body movements, and eye contact
   - an expressive tone of voice

C. SPEAK Narrate your experience in groups or for the whole class. As you listen to your classmates, write down similes and metaphors that you especially liked. At the end of the activity, share these with the whole class. Refer to the Self-Assessment checklist below before you begin.

CHECK AND REFLECT

A. CHECK Think about the Unit Assignment as you complete the Self-Assessment checklist.

SELF-ASSESSMENT		
Yes	No	
☐	☐	I was able to speak fluently about the topic.
☐	☐	My group and class understood me.
☐	☐	I used the correct negative prefixes for adjectives.
☐	☐	I used the active voice and the passive voice appropriately.
☐	☐	I used similes and metaphors to make my language more interesting.
☐	☐	I emphasized words in the correct places to express my meaning.

B. REFLECT Discuss these questions with a partner.

What is something new you learned in this unit?

 Look back at the Unit Question. Is your answer different now than when you started this unit? If yes, how is it different? Why?

Circle the words you learned in this unit.

Nouns
boundary
consciousness
fragment
function 🔑 AWL
incident
insight AWL
outburst
perception AWL
recovery 🔑 AWL
sentiment
structure 🔑 AWL

Verbs
gesticulate
imitate
persist AWL
regain
reveal 🔑 AWL

Adjectives
adequate 🔑 AWL
external AWL
fascinating
intense 🔑 AWL
invisible AWL

overall 🔑 AWL
tangible
tranquil

Adverbs
invariably AWL

🔑 Oxford 3000™ words
AWL Academic Word List

Check (✓) the skills you learned. If you need more work on a skill, refer to the page(s) in parentheses.

LISTENING	●	I can make inferences. (p. 59)
VOCABULARY	●	I can use negative prefixes. (p. 65)
GRAMMAR	●	I can use the passive voice. (p. 67)
PRONUNCIATION	●	I can use emphatic word stress. (p. 69)
SPEAKING	●	I can use figurative language. (p. 71)
LEARNING OUTCOME	●	I can develop a narrative incorporating figurative language that chronologically details an incident of language loss or an inability to communicate.

UNIT 4

Personal Space

LISTENING ● recognizing organizational cues
VOCABULARY ● words with multiple meanings
GRAMMAR ● conditionals
PRONUNCIATION ● thought groups
SPEAKING ● giving advice

LEARNING OUTCOME

Role-play a talk show focused on identifying and solving conflicts centered on issues of personal space.

Unit QUESTION

How do you make a space your own?

PREVIEW THE UNIT

Ⓐ Discuss these questions with your classmates.

What places or spaces do you have that you consider "yours"? How do other people know that these spaces belong to you?

What are some differences in the way different groups, such as males, female, adults, or children personalize their space?

Look at the photo. Do you think the people who live in the house have made the space their own? Why?

Ⓑ Discuss the Unit Question above with your classmates.

🔊 Listen to Level 9(CM), Track 26 to hear other answers.

77

C Look at the pictures of different kinds of space. What does each space tell you about the person? Share your ideas with a partner.

D Work in a group. Think of one of your personal spaces. Take turns describing your space and explaining what it shows about you.

My room is usually a little messy, but it is filled with things I really enjoy. In one corner is a pile of sports equipment: my tennis racket, some balls, a Frisbee, and a baseball glove. On the wall are posters of movies I really like. I've got a lot of CDs on the shelves. There's a plant on my windowsill.

LISTENING 1 | Environmental Psychology

VOCABULARY

Here are some words and phrases from Listening 1. Read the sentences. Circle the answer that best matches the meaning of each bold word or phrase.

1. **Gender** differences between boys and girls can be seen at an early age.
   a. classification by age
   b. classification by sex
   c. classification by name

2. To work with your partner on this dialog, sit in chairs that are face-to-face or in ones that are **adjacent** so you can communicate easily.
   a. next to each other
   b. away from the door
   c. far from each other

3. People usually **affiliate with** others who are similar to themselves. They like to feel that they belong to a group of like-minded friends.
   a. connect to
   b. are curious about
   c. are afraid of

4. The teachers are going to **engage in** a discussion on social psychology, so I'd like to stay and hear what they have to say.
   a. schedule
   b. take part in
   c. call off

5. He keeps all of his **belongings**, including his books and clothes, in one small cabinet in his dorm room.
   a. things you want
   b. things you don't want
   c. things you own

6. It's **remarkable** how often people will choose to sit at the same table in a restaurant, even when better tables are available.
   a. very interesting
   b. very difficult to believe
   c. very uncomfortable

7. Territorial behavior, or wanting to protect a personal space, is **ingrained in** us, and it is hard to change our attitude.
   a. all around
   b. unfamiliar to
   c. deeply a part of

8. When my little sister **invades** my room, she throws her toys all over my bed.
   a. forgets about; ignores
   b. protects; takes good care of
   c. marches into; enters by force

9. Most pizza places only deliver within a three-mile **radius**.
   a. circular area
   b. city center
   c. diameter

10. Please **refrain from** using your cell phone in class because it distracts other students.
    a. think about
    b. continue
    c. avoid

11. They prefer to commute to work in the city every day but live in a **suburban** area, because life is less stressful there.
    a. in a city
    b. near a city
    c. very far from a city

12. Although visitors are not likely to enter a house without knocking, they are **moderately** likely to stop by for a visit without being invited. It happens sometimes.
    a. always
    b. a little
    c. very

PREVIEW LISTENING 1

Environmental Psychology

You are going to listen to an excerpt from a lecture by Dr. Traci Craig, a psychology professor at the University of Idaho. It will introduce you to the field of environmental psychology.

Behavioral psychology is the study of how humans react to stimuli from outside and within themselves. *Educational psychology* is the study of how humans learn. Look at the pictures below. What do you think *environmental psychology* is? Write a short definition.

_____

_____

_____

Tip for Success

Learning the special vocabulary of academic fields will help you understand discussions and lectures and make you more comfortable communicating at school. Keep lists of vocabulary you learn in different subjects.

LISTEN FOR MAIN IDEAS

 Level 9(CM)
Track 27

A. Listen to the lecture. Take notes to complete the main ideas in the outline.

Tip Critical Thinking

In Activity A, you will complete an outline. **Outlining** is one way of breaking down information into its component parts.

I. Environmental psychology

    A. Definition: _____

       _____

    B. Areas the lecture will focus on:

       1. _____

       2. _____

       3. _____

II. Male and female _____ behavior

    A. Feelings of invasion

        1. Face-to-face invasion (males)

        2. _____ invasion (females)

    B. Placement of belongings

        1. The _____ study

        2. Placement of _____

    C. Exploring territories on bikes

        1. Smaller territories for girls

        2. Larger territories for boys

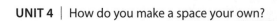

a server and customer in a restaurant

    D. Touching _____ in _____

III. Eye contact: Post office experiment

    A. _____ likely to make eye

       contact in a _____

    B. _____ likely to make eye

       contact in a _____

IV. Visual intrusion and privacy—stressful places

    A. Visual intrusion—to see and be seen

        1. Restaurants

        2. _____

    B. Privacy—dorm rooms

B. Use your notes from the outline in Activity A to write answers to these questions. Compare your answers with a partner.

1. What is environmental psychology?

_____

2. In what ways does Dr. Craig believe males and females are similar or different in their territorial behavior?

_____

3. According to Dr. Craig, what is the connection between eye contact and personal space?

_____

4. What effects can a feeling of lack of privacy have on an individual?

_____

LISTEN FOR DETAILS

Level 9(CM)
Track 28

A. Read the statements. Then listen again. Write *T* (true) or *F* (false). Compare your answers with a partner.

____ 1. Men are more offended by someone sitting adjacent to them than someone sitting across from them.

____ 2. Males and females often miscommunicate because they are both competitive.

____ 3. The statement "Women are expected to affiliate" means women feel they have to make contact with someone they sit next to.

____ 4. In a large lecture class, the majority of students sit in the same seat all semester.

____ 5. Visitors to a man's office will touch his belongings displayed on the desk more freely than they would if the office belonged to a woman.

____ 6. In the jacket study, people moved a jacket that clearly belonged to a woman, but refrained from moving one that belonged to a man.

____ 7. Territorial behavior does not begin until we are teenagers.

____ 8. Even at a young age, females explore larger territories than males.

____ 9. Touching your plate in a restaurant is a sign of marking the plate as your own.

____ 10. It is more acceptable and expected for people to make eye contact in a post office in a large city than in a small town.

Q WHAT DO YOU THINK?

Discuss the questions in a group.

1. How do the details that you marked as true in the previous exercise fit your own actions or your observations of others? Do you always choose to sit in the same chair in class, for example?

2. Has Dr. Craig convinced you that males and females have very different reactions to personal space? Why or why not?

3. In what ways do you think the rules for respecting personal space and personalizing territories vary in different countries and cultures?

Listening Skill   Recognizing organizational cues

Organizational cues are words or phrases a speaker uses to signal the type of information that follows. Recognizing organizational cues can help you predict what speakers will say next.

Organizational cues	What they signal	Examples
most importantly, in fact, actually, what we will focus on here is, I want to stress	importance, emphasis	What we will focus on here is a definition of territoriality.
for example, such as, for instance, specifically, in particular, that is	examples, illustrations	There are many ways to invade someone's space. For example, if you . . .
furthermore, in addition, moreover, besides, additionally, also	additional support or evidence	Women try to talk to those sitting next to them. In addition, they feel they have to affiliate with them.
now let's turn to, moving on, let's now look at, related to that	shifting topics	Now let's turn to the statistical evidence.
in short, to sum up, in conclusion, we've seen that, in the end	conclusions	In short, gender affects our sense of space.

Level 9(CM)
Track 29

A. Listen to this excerpt from Listening 1 and write down the six organizational cues that you hear. Then work with a partner and discuss the reasons the lecturer used them in each case.

1. _____

2. _____

3. _____

4. _____

5. _____

6. _____

Level 9(CM)
Track 30

B. Listen to the beginnings of these sentences and circle the correct ending for each, based on the organizational cues that you hear.

1. a students who take the time to put up posters feel more at home.
   b. their attendance in class is better and their grades are higher.

2. a. we found some posts by teenagers about how they got out of doing some school assignments.
   b. we found some detailed resumes of businessmen.

3. a. women don't usually consider their cars as a personal space to spend time on.
   b. it is believed that most men would rather watch football on their day off than go out to eat.

4. a. our car is just one piece of evidence of who we are.
   b. a car is enough information on which to base an opinion of a person.

5. a. eye contact does not appear to be a gender-related issue.
   b. men usually put a jacket on a seat in front of them rather than next to them.

6. a. staring at people is considered inappropriate and makes them feel uncomfortable.
   b. psychologists use all of this information to help people understand why they behave the way they do.

VOCABULARY

Here are some words from Listening 2. Read the paragraphs. Then write each bold word next to the correct definition.

Each of our actions and all of the spaces within our **domain** say something about us, whether we make those statements on purpose or not. Our personality **traits** are revealed by the ways we behave and the things we use to define our spaces. Anyone who spends time with us usually can walk away with a **profile** of us based on the things we own and the way we act with others. Although this information may provide **clues** to help others judge our personalities, it can also mislead them if one action or object makes them jump to the wrong conclusion. Then they have to **modify** their perception and try again to figure us out.

Two traits of the human personality that psychologists use as a **framework** to study human behavior are *introversion* and *extroversion*. Through observations and experiments, they try to **clarify** the differences between groups with these traits. An **introvert** generally prefers not to make eye contact and prefers to be alone, while an **extrovert** seeks opportunities to invite people in and start up a conversation. An introvert does not want to make eye contact because he wants to maintain his own personal space. He enters a room **tentatively** and might stand in the corner observing others before talking to them. Privacy is **crucial** to him. In contrast, an extrovert invites people to learn more about her; she may quickly **propose** getting together for some kind of activity even if she has just met someone. She may even make her private life more widely known in a virtual environment such as a website or a Facebook page.

1. _____ *(v.)* to change slightly

2. _____ *(v.)* to suggest a plan or an action

3. _____ *(n.)* a quiet person not interested in spending time with others

4. _____ *(n.)* pieces of information that help solve a puzzle

5. _____ *(v.)* to make something clear and easy to understand

6. _____ *(n.)* a description of somebody or something that gives useful information

7. _____ *(adv.)* without confidence or certainty

8. _____ *(n.)* qualities of a person's character

9. _____ (n.) a lively, confident person who enjoys being with others

10. _____ (n.) an area owned or ruled by a person or government

11. _____ (adj.) extremely important

12. _____ (n.) a system of ideas or rules

PREVIEW LISTENING 2

What Your Stuff Says About You

You are going to listen to part of a radio interview and call-in show from NPR's *Talk of the Nation*. On the show, Dr. Sam Gosling, a psychology professor, discusses his book, *Snoop: What Your Stuff Says About You.*

Dr. Gosling says that he looks for information about people in many places—and that he uses the word *places* very broadly, to refer not only to physical areas. Talk with a partner. What kinds of places or things do you think Dr. Gosling might be interested in?

LISTEN FOR MAIN IDEAS

Level 9(CM)
Track 31

A. Read the questions. Then listen to the interview. Write short answers. Compare your ideas with a partner.

1. What are some places Dr. Gosling snoops around that reveal a great deal about people?

   _____

   _____

2. Does Dr. Gosling believe that people are always correct in the conclusions they come to about the possessions and actions of others? Why or why not?

   _____

   _____

3. How does psychology play a role in figuring out "what your stuff says about you"?

   _____

   _____

LISTEN FOR DETAILS

Level 9(CM)
Track 32

B. Listen again. Complete the sentences.

1. Two personal objects the host, Neal Conan, has in his office are

   _____ .

2. In addition to the actual objects people display, Dr. Gosling says it is

   important to notice _____ .

3. The objects Dr. Gosling indicates as revealing the most about people are

   _____ .

4. One example of an oral or virtual environment would be

   _____ .

5. The two personality types the psychologist often refers to are

   _____ .

6. The experiment mentioned in the interview that affected people's

   impressions of others involved _____ .

7. When we are asked, "What does this stuff say about someone?"

   Dr. Gosling believes that the mistake we make is that we might

   _____ .

8. In the end, Dr. Gosling decides that the adjective he would use to describe

   the host, Neal Conan, is _____ .

 WHAT DO YOU THINK?

A. Discuss the questions in a group.

1. Do you agree with Dr. Gosling that we are all natural-born snoops? Why or why not? Use examples from your own life to support your opinion.

2. Look around your classroom. What conclusions might Dr. Gosling draw from what he could see there?

B. Think about both Listening 1 and Listening 2 as you discuss the questions.

1. What different answers might Dr. Gosling and Dr. Craig have to this question that was sent in to *Talk of the Nation*: "What would you say about people who do not include personal items in their offices or cars?"

2. What other professions would be interested in the findings of psychologists and their studies of personal space and privacy? Why?

Vocabulary Skill	Words with multiple meanings

Many words in English have more than one meaning, so you cannot assume that the one definition you know will fit every situation. For example, the following definitions can be found in the dictionary for the word *chair*.

---

chair /tʃɛr/ *noun, verb*
- *noun* **1** [C] a piece of furniture for one person to sit on, with a back, a seat, and four legs: *a table and chairs* ♦ *Sit on your chair!* ♦ *an old man asleep in a chair* (= an ARMCHAIR) ⊃ picture on page 235 ⊃ see also ARMCHAIR, DECK CHAIR, EASY CHAIR, HIGH CHAIR, MUSICAL CHAIRS, ROCKING CHAIR, WHEELCHAIR **2** [C] = CHAIRMAN, CHAIRPERSON **3** [C] the person in charge of a department in a university: *He is the chair of philosophy at Stanford.* **4 the chair** [sing.] (*informal*) = THE ELECTRIC CHAIR
- *verb* ~ **sth** to act as the chairman or chairwoman of a meeting, discussion, etc.: *Who's chairing the meeting?*

The dictionary can help you choose the correct definition if you:
1. check the part of speech to eliminate any definitions that do not fit the grammar of the sentence.
2. check the first definition, which is usually the most common definition.
3. look at the sample sentences to determine which best fits the context.

The third step would confirm that the best definition of *chair* in the sentence "She is the chair of the psychology department" is the third definition listed, "the person in charge of a department in a university."

All dictionary entries are from the *Oxford Advanced American Dictionary for learners of English* © Oxford University Press 2011.

A. Read the sentences and write the letter of the correct definition of the underlined words. Use the context and a dictionary to help you.

_____ 1. They didn't understand that the jacket was a <u>marker</u> to save a seat.

_____ 2. She bought a <u>marker</u> to write her name in her books.

    a. *(n.)* a type of pen that draws thick lines

    b. *(n.)* an object or sign that shows the position of something

    c. *(n.)* a sign that something exists or that shows what it is like

_____ 3. In the video game <u>Space</u> Invasion, players engage in wars between the planets.

_____ 4. We try to respect the desk, office <u>space</u>, and seating arrangements.

_____ 5. Can you <u>space</u> the chairs so that they don't touch one another?

    d. *(n.)* an area or room

    e. *(n.)* an unused or empty area

    f. *(n.)* the area around the Earth

    g. *(n.)* a period of time

    h. *(v.)* to arrange things with areas or gaps between

_____ 6. Did you <u>mean</u> to leave your jacket on my desk?

_____ 7. The <u>mean</u> number of students who take that psychology class each year is 75.

_____ 8. Radius can <u>mean</u> one-half of a diameter or an area surrounding a point.

    i. *(v.)* to intend to say or do something

    j. *(v.)* to have something as a meaning

    k. *(adj.)* average

    l. *(adj.)* (of people or their behavior) unkind

___ 9. She couldn't <u>refrain</u> from trying to make eye contact with him.

___ 10. The teacher said the same <u>refrain</u> again and again: "Keep your eyes to yourself."

  m. *(n.)* a part of a poem or song that is repeated

  n. *(n.)* a comment or complaint that is often repeated

  o. *(v.)* to stop yourself from doing something

B. Use your dictionary to look up the definitions for one of these words. Copy three definitions and label them *a*, *b*, and *c*. Then write three sentences that reflect the different definitions for each of your words, as in Activity A.

contact	place	stress	stuff	type

Word: _____

Definitions:

a. _____

b. _____

c. _____

Sentences:

a. _____

_____

b. _____

_____

c. _____

_____

C. Take turns reading one of your sentences from Activity B to a partner. See if your partner can choose the correct definition of the word for that sentence.

Grammar | Conditionals

The verbs in conditional sentences show:

- the time frame (present, present/future, or past).
- whether the conditions are real (true) or unreal (not true; imaginary).

Present/future real conditionals: There is a real possibility the condition will happen, or it can, should, or might happen.

If clause = present tense form

Result = *will, can, might, should* + base verb

[If he **wants** to make friends, he **should join** a club.
He **will not enjoy** parties if he **is** an introvert.

Present/future unreal conditionals: The condition is not true now, so the results are not true either.

If clause = past tense form

Result = *would, might* + base verb

[If she **wanted** to reveal more about her personality, she **would display** photos.
He **might sit** at the front of the classroom if he **weren't** so shy.

Past unreal conditionals: The condition was not true before; the result in the past or the present is not true either.

If clause = past perfect form

Result = *would, could, might* + base verb (present results) *would have, could have, might have* + past participle (past results)

[If they **had asked** everyone about painting the room, no one **would be** angry now.
If everyone **had contributed** some money, we **could have redecorated**.

Tip for Success

In present unreal conditionals, the form *were* is used instead of *was* for all speakers: *If I* **were** *rich, I'd give more money to charity.* However, in informal situations, you may hear people use **was**.

A. Read the conditional sentence. Then circle the correct conclusion that you can draw.

1. If I'd seen him, I would've said "hello."
   a. I saw the man.
   b. I didn't say "hello."

2. She will probably be standing in a crowd of friends if she is an extrovert.
   a. She isn't standing in a crowd of friends now.
   b. She may be an extrovert, but I'm not sure.

3. If privacy had been so important to her, she wouldn't have left the door open.
   a. Privacy was important to her.
   b. She left the door open.

4. Shouldn't you label your stuff if you want us to know it's yours?
   a. We know it's your stuff.
   b. Your stuff is not labeled.

5. If he weren't so afraid of making new friends, he'd hang out in the library more.
   a. He doesn't hang out in the library much now.
   b. He isn't afraid of making new friends.

6. I would be sitting on that chair if he hadn't left his coat on it.
   a. I am sitting on the chair.
   b. He left his coat on the chair.

B. Complete the sentences. Then compare them with a partner. Check each other's verb forms.

1. If I had known you were an extrovert, _____.

2. If I could redecorate my room, _____.

3. If I am going into a new classroom for the first time, _____.

4. If I didn't want to share my space, _____.

5. _____ he might lock the door.

6. _____ I would get a roommate.

7. _____ I wouldn't have gone home early.

8. _____ I would have been angry.

Thought groups are meaningful phrases (groups of words) or clauses (sentence parts that have a subject and a verb) that express an idea. Just as writers use punctuation to separate sentence elements, speakers use intonation and pauses to help listeners process what they are hearing.

If listeners make the wrong connections between your words, this can lead to an error in understanding.

Level 9(CM)
Track 33

For example, read and listen to these two sentences. Notice how the different thought groups (indicated with slashes /) change the meaning.

> The psychologist / said the lecturer / tries to understand social behavior.
> "The psychologist," said the lecturer, "tries to understand social behavior."
>
> The psychologist said / the lecturer / tries to understand social behavior.
> The psychologist said, "The lecturer tries to understand social behavior."

To make effective thought groups, remember to:

- divide sentences into meaningful units (don't separate an adjective and a noun, for example).
- put the most stress on the final key word in each thought group.
- end a thought group with a slight fall or a fall-rise in intonation.
- pause slightly at the end of each thought group.
- not drop your pitch too low until the end of a sentence.

Level 9(CM)
Track 34

A. Listen to this excerpt from Listening 2. Mark the thought groups you hear by drawing lines between them. Compare your work with a partner. The first sentence is done for you.

Dr. Gosling: That's right / because it's really important / you know / if I had one wish / one wish in the world / it would be that one clue / told you something / about a person. If you had a stuffed teddy on your bed it meant something you know. But the world is more complicated than that. So unfortunately it doesn't work like that because there are many reasons why we might have say a stuffed animal on our bed or something like that. And so really you can't use a codebook approach where x means y. What you have to do is you have to build up a picture piece by piece and sometimes you only have a very little piece and you have to hold your view very tentatively. But that will that will guide your search for more information.

Tip for Success

As you become a more proficient speaker, try to make your thought groups longer so your speaking is less choppy and more fluent.

B. With your partner, take turns reading one of the following sentences in each set. See if your partner can identify which sentence, *a* or *b*, you are reading.

1. a. So if we really wanted to understand kids, that's the question we would ask.
   b. So, if we really wanted to understand, kids, that's the question we would ask.

2. a. "The lecturer," said the students, "couldn't explain environmental psychology very well."
   b. The lecturer said, "The students couldn't explain environmental psychology very well."

3. a. This is a way of maintaining space. In a rural area, you often feel you have enough space.
   b. This is a way of maintaining space in a rural area. You often feel you have enough space.

4. a. "The psychologist," claims my sister, "is an extrovert," but I don't believe it.
   b. The psychologist claims my sister is an extrovert, but I don't believe it.

Speaking Skill   Giving advice

Knowing how to make suggestions and give advice without sounding pushy or demanding is an important conversational skill.

In each column in the chart, the expressions are listed from the weakest to the strongest forms of advice.

Advice with modals in the present/future	Advice with modals in the past	Advice using *if*	Other expressions
You might want to . . .	You could have . . .	If I were you, I would . . .	Why don't you . . . ?
You can/could . . .	You might have . . .	(Notice that we use *if I were you* to show that the speaker is not really that person.)	Have you thought about . . . ?
You should . . .	You should have . . .		Whatever you do, don't . . . !
You ought to . . .	You had to . . .		Whatever you do, make sure to . . . !
You had better (You'd better) . . .			
You must (not) . . .			

Tip for Success

Suggest and *recommend* are followed by *that* + the person you are giving advice to + a base verb: *I suggested that he move in. She recommended that he talk more.*

A. Work in a group. Take turns reading the problems below and giving advice to the speaker according to the situation. Share and discuss your sentences in a group.

A: *My sister thinks I'm a slob because I don't wash or clean my car.*

B: *I think you should clean it if you want to change her attitude.*

C: *Yeah, if I were you, I'd clean it. Otherwise she won't want to go anywhere with you.*

D: *Why don't you ask a couple of friends to help you clean it?*

1. People make fun of me for wearing crazy clothes.

2. My room is so full of stuff I can't get any work done.

3. Our neighbors are going to build a tall fence around their property.

4. I'd like to ask my instructor for help, but I feel too shy.

5. I sat next to someone on the subway this morning, and he gave me a terrible look.

6. My roommate is always using my computer.

B. Work with a partner. Role-play a conversation with a friend who is moving into an empty office space for his or her first job. Take turns asking for and giving advice on ways to personalize the space and mark it as his or her own.

Unit Assignment | Role-play a talk show

In this section, you will role-play a talk show. As you prepare your role-play, think about the Unit Question, "How do you make a space your own?" and refer to the Self-Assessment checklist on page 98.

For alternative unit assignments, see the *Q: Skills for Success Teacher's Handbook*.

CONSIDER THE IDEAS

Listen to this excerpt from a radio call-in show, in which a psychologist helps two college roommates who need advice about sharing a space. Discuss the questions below in a group.

1. What is the main issue that is causing the problem between the roommates? What kind of advice do you think Dr. Hill will offer?

2. Talk about a time when your own feelings about personal space caused you to come into conflict with someone else. What happened? How did you resolve the conflict? What did you learn from it?

PREPARE AND SPEAK

A. GATHER IDEAS In a group, talk about the kinds of conflicts that can develop when people live together. Brainstorm different types of relationships, the conflicts that might come up between people regarding personal space, and solutions. Write your ideas in the chart.

Relationship	Conflict	Advice / Solution

B. ORGANIZE IDEAS In pairs or groups of three, write a script for a role-play of a talk show, using one of the conflicts you came up with in Activity A. One or two of you will play the role(s) of someone with a problem related to space. One of you will be the expert who offers advice and solutions. Follow these steps.

1. Introduce yourselves and describe your situation and relationship.

2. Explain the problem or conflict over personal space.

3. Offer solutions and advice, both real and imaginary.

4. Give your reactions to the advice.

 **Tip for Success**

In order to avoid monotone intonation or flat speaking, make sure to show enthusiasm and interest by stressing key words so they stand out.

C. SPEAK Practice your role-play in your group, and then present it to the class. Ask the class if they can think of any other solutions to the problem you presented. Refer to the Self-Assessment checklist below before you begin.

CHECK AND REFLECT

A. CHECK Think about the Unit Assignment as you complete the Self-Assessment checklist.

Yes	No	SELF-ASSESSMENT
☐	☐	I was able to speak fluently about the topic.
☐	☐	My group and class understood me.
☐	☐	I used conditionals correctly.
☐	☐	I used vocabulary from the unit to express my ideas.
☐	☐	I phrased my sentences in thought groups to help my speech sound more natural.
☐	☐	I was able to give advice.

B. REFLECT Discuss these questions with a partner.

What is something new you learned in this unit?

 Look back at the Unit Question. Is your answer different now than when you started this unit? If yes, how is it different? Why?

Track Your Success

Circle the words and phrases you learned in this unit.

Nouns
belongings
clue
domain AWL
extrovert
framework AWL
gender AWL
introvert
profile 🔑
radius
trait

Verbs
clarify AWL
invade
modify AWL
propose 🔑

Adjectives
adjacent AWL
crucial 🔑 AWL
remarkable 🔑
suburban

Adverbs
moderately
tentatively

Phrases
affiliate with
ingrained in

Phrasal Verbs
engage in 🔑
refrain from

🔑 Oxford 3000™ words
AWL Academic Word List

Check (✓) the skills you learned. If you need more work on a skill, refer to the page(s) in parentheses.

LISTENING	●	I can recognize organizational cues. (p. 84)
VOCABULARY	●	I can use words with multiple meanings. (p. 89)
GRAMMAR	●	I can use conditionals. (p. 92)
PRONUNCIATION	●	I can use thought groups. (p. 94)
SPEAKING	●	I can give advice. (p. 95)
LEARNING OUTCOME	●	I can role-play a talk show focused on identifying and solving conflicts centered on issues of personal space.

OXFORD
UNIVERSITY PRESS

Oxford University Press is a department of the University of Oxford.
It furthers the University's objective of excellence in research, scholarship,
and education by publishing worldwide. Oxford is a registered trade mark of
Oxford University Press in the UK and in certain other countries.

Published in Canada by
Oxford University Press
8 Sampson Mews, Suite 204,
Don Mills, Ontario M3C 0H5 Canada

www.oupcanada.com

First Edition published in 2014
ISBN: 978-0-19-901353-1   ILSC English Communication 9: Q Skills for Success

Previously published as part of:
Q Skills for Success Listening and Speaking 5 Student's Book
© Oxford University Press 2011

Q: Skills for Success was originally published in English in 2011.
This edition is published by arrangement with Oxford University Press,
Great Clarendon Street, Oxford 0X2 6DP, United Kingdom.

Oxford University Press is committed to our environment.
Wherever possible, our books are printed on paper which comes from
responsible sources.

Printed and bound in the United States of America

1 2 3 4 — 17 16 15 14

ACKNOWLEDGEMENTS

The Publisher would like to thank the following for their kind permission to reproduce photographs: Back cover: ILSC Education Group; p. 2 © John Francis/CORBIS; p. 4 (l) Roger Allyn Lee/SuperStock; (r) F1online/Thinkstock; p. 6 © FLPA/Terry Whittaker/age fotostock; p. 11 (t) © Spring Images/Alamy; (b) © RubberBall/Alamy; p. 22 © Jim West/Alamy; p. 26 © Lourens Smak/Alamy; p. 28 (tl–br) © Alex Slobodkin/iStockphoto; © Ibushuev/iStockphoto; © Gawrav Sinha/iStockphoto; © N_design/iStockphoto; Rtimages/Shutterstock; p. 30 Jb Reed/Bloomberg via Getty Images; p. 37 Maneesh Agnihotri/The India Today Group/Getty Images; p. 38 ADEK BERRY/AFP/Getty Images; p. 41 © Roger Ressmeyer/CORBIS; p. 43 © Whitemann/Corbis; p. 47 Blend Images - John Lund/Marc Romanelli/Getty Images; p. 48 © moodboard/Corbis; p. 52 DON EMMERT/AFP/Getty Images; p. 56 © My Stroke of Insight, Inc.; p. 59 (l) © LOOK Die Bildagentur der Fotografen GmbH/Alamy; (r) © Richard Green/Alamy; p. 62 Library of Congress - LC-USZ62-78999; p. 66 © MGM/Zuma Press; p. 70 Yuri Arcurs/Shutterstock; p. 73 Yellow Dog Productions/Getty Images; p. 76 Wayne Barrett & Anne/All Canada Photos/SuperStock; p. 81 MedicalRF.com/Getty Images; p. 82 Tara Moore/Getty Images; p. 87 Thomas Northcut/Thinkstock; p. 96 Sheltered Images/SuperStock

Illustrations by: p. 4 Stacy Merlin; p. 7 Stacy Merlin; p. 28 Stacy Merlin; p. 54 Stuart Bradford; p 78 Greg Paprocki; p. 81 Greg Paprocki; p. 97 Greg Paprocki